THE CHAMPIONSHIPS
WIMBLEDON
Official Annual 1997

JOHN PARSONS

Photographs by
CLIVE BRUNSKILL, GARY M. PRIOR
and STU FORSTER
of Allsport Photographic

Publisher
RICHARD POULTER

Production Manager
STEVEN PALMER

Publishing Development Manager
SIMON MAURICE

Business Development Manager
SIMON SANDERSON

Art Editor
STEVE SMALL

Managing Editor
PETER LOVERING

Publicity and promotion
CLARE KRISTENSEN

Photography
CLIVE BRUNSKILL
GARY M. PRIOR
STU FORSTER

Photo Research, Allsport
ELAINE LOBO
KER ROBERTSON

This first edition published in 1997 by Hazleton Publishing Ltd,
3 Richmond Hill, Richmond, Surrey TW10 6RE

ISBN: 1-874557-42-X

Printed in England by Ebenezer Baylis & Son Ltd, Worcester

Colour reproduction by Adroit Photo Litho Ltd, Birmingham

Results tables are reproduced by courtesy of
The All England Lawn Tennis Club

This book is produced with the assistance of Nikon (UK) Limited

FOREWORD

It is always a pleasure to write the Foreword for the Annual, particularly this year when everything finished so well after the terrible weather of the first week.

In the short term, we all remember the worst weather for The Championships in living memory: the two weeks with two days washed out and rain on seven days. However, there was the compensation of a very successful and happy middle Sunday. Everybody takes credit for that triumph. The players – not least our British stars – did us proud on the middle Sunday and the organisation and effort of all who work here gave over 31,000 fans a great day.

But I feel the long-term memory will be the opening ceremony of No. 1 Court and the birth of the new stadium. The champions who paraded on court that day have given, and are still giving, great pleasure to tennis fans around the world. The ambience of the court and the landscaped hillside give The Championships a new dimension. We have that indefinable excitement and tradition of the Centre Court and now we have the younger, fresher sibling to take us into the 21st century.

There was also the excitement of great tennis: of new stars

making their reputations and current champions establishing their greatness. How we enjoyed the talent of the No. 1 seeds and singles winners, Martina Hingis and Pete Sampras. His awesome display of only dropping service twice in 118 service games is a record that will stand the test of time. For the British, the success of the men was also a special pleasure.

The semi-finals of the singles epitomised the world of tennis today with all the eight players coming from different countries. Europe was well represented by Michael Stich from Germany, Cedric Pioline from France, Martina Hingis from Switzerland, Jana Novotna from the Czech Republic and Arantxa Sanchez Vicario from Spain. Finally, Todd Woodbridge and Mark Woodforde's fifth Wimbledon doubles title rounded off a great fortnight on the Centre Court.

These highlights and many others are represented in the Annual. I hope you enjoy the record of the 111th Championships as much as I do.

John Curry
Chairman of The All England Lawn Tennis & Croquet Club
and the Committee of Management of The Championships

INTRODUCTION

IMBLEDON presented a handsome new appearance in 1997. The Centre Court looked the same, of course. That, surely, is sacrosanct. On its north side, though, there were no longer the towering cranes and other evidence of construction which had greeted visitors in the two previous years. There, bold and welcoming, was the new No. 1 Court, with its 11,000 seats resting above restaurants, shops and a whole range of other facilities. Some of the greatest former champions, all of them at least three-times winners, from Rod Laver and Margaret Court to Boris Becker and Pete Sampras, were eager to add a touch of nostalgia from the past to the admiration for the present in a new arena built to sustain Wimbledon into an exciting future.

There was also the new permanent broadcast centre, offering the most modern facilities for Wimbledon to be enjoyed by listeners and viewers in 167 countries, plus a masterpiece of modern landscaping, complete with waterfall and an inviting new picnic area. It all brought reality to the promise by the All England Club that it would preserve the image of lawn tennis in an English country garden, amid the modern developments and comfort which both the public and the players demand and deserve.

What, though, of the expectations about The Championships themselves in 1997? It was, according to general consent, likely to be an even more wide-open contest for the men's singles title than the year before when, for the first time, two players who had originally been unseeded fought their way into the final. Yet the most intriguing question was whether anyone could stop Martina Hingis, who had lost only one match earlier in the year, from becoming the youngest women's singles champion at Wimbledon this century. Jana Novotna, with her attacking game so wonderfully suited to the grass, had the best chance, many felt, including a large number of the players.

Novotna's prospects were boosted by the news, just before the seedings were announced, that Steffi Graf, whom she should have beaten in the 1993 final, had suddenly undergone knee surgery after losing in the semi-finals of the French Open and would not be able to defend the title she had won for a seventh time in 1996.

Far left: The changing landscape of Wimbledon, now that the new No. 1 Court, on the right of the picture, is part of the scene.

Left: Chris Evert admires the salver presented to her during the opening ceremony, which was only briefly delayed by the first of all too many showers which passed over Wimbledon in the first week.

Everyone in Britain was keen to see for themselves how well Hingis's game had broadened and matured since Wimbledon '96 when, even then, at 15, she showed more than a hint of budding greatness in the second set of her fourth-round defeat by Graf. They knew, of course, through the media how she had dominated the women's game in the first six months of the year but this was to be her biggest test, especially as she had hardly disguised her misgivings about playing on a surface she felt suited her horse more than her.

Yet there were also three other teenagers pressing hard for attention: Iva Majoli, 19, the only player to have beaten Hingis in 1997, in the final at Roland Garros; Anna Kournikova, only just 16, who had fast been replacing Gabriela Sabatini as the most photographed player on the women's tour; and newcomer Venus Williams, just 17, the tall and strong black Californian, who had filled more column inches worldwide before her father even allowed her to start competing seriously than many players collect in a lifetime. Would Williams, for instance, go ahead with the idea she expressed in Paris of replacing the mass of white beads in her hair with purple and green ones, the All England Club colours?

There were also Arantxa Sanchez Vicario, so close to being the champion but runner-up to Graf in the two previous years, second-seeded Monica Seles, courageously trying to overcome worries about her father's health, and others to consider.

Among the men, no one could realistically question the status of Pete Sampras as the best player but indifferent form since winning his first 17 matches of the year made some question his stamina and therefore promote the prospects of Yevgeny Kafelnikov and defending champion Richard Krajicek, and also consider whether Goran Ivanisevic might at last show the mental persistence and resilience needed to win.

All this plus the ever-growing expectations of Tim Henman, Britain's first player to break into the top 20 for more than a decade, despite the way he had needed longer than expected to lift his game back to a peak after elbow surgery in March. There were equally high hopes of Greg Rusedski with his immediate chance to set things rolling with a first-round match against Mark Philippoussis. Wimbledon '97 was ready for the off.

NIKON F5: 8 FRAMES PER SECOND WITH

WORLD RECORD.

3D COLOUR MATRIX METERING SYSTEM • 1005-PIXEL EXPOSURE METERING SYSTEM
5 AREA DYNAMIC AUTOFOCUS • 1st SELF-DIAGNOSTIC SHUTTER CONTROL

FOCUS TRACKING.

F5. STEP AHEAD. *Nikon*

pete SAMPRAS

Anyone who bets against Pete Sampras at Wimbledon 'must be mad', said one coach to another aspirant for the title when the 1997 prospects were being assessed.

For although a year earlier Sampras had been forced to give up the crown he had worn so confidently for three years when he lost a magnificent quarter-final against Richard Krajicek, few still questioned the American's reputation as the best player on grass.

Apart from a wonderfully effective and varied serve, based as much on guile and control as power, his grinding groundstrokes and impressive mobility about the court mean there have been times, not least at Wimbledon, when his almost faultless game has been too good to be fully appreciated.

'What I like most is walking through the gates at Wimbledon because there's a certain aura, a certain history, that you don't really feel anywhere else,' says Sampras. 'Wimbledon was the one I'd always dreamed about winning when I was young.'

USA   Age: 25
World Ranking: 1

goran IVANISEVIC

As in previous years, the lean, left-handed Croatian went into The Championships with many still wondering how, with his instinctively aggressive, big-serving game, ideally suited for grass, he had never done better than finishing as runner-up in 1992 and 1994.

Ivanisevic himself found it easy to supply the answer. 'At Wimbledon you have to play seven best-of-five-set matches in a row and that's not easy,' said the ace-king, who added, 'When I stay calm and focused I'm unbeatable. I'm always dangerous but I don't always know for what.'

A flamboyant character, Ivanisevic slammed a door in his apartment without looking what he was doing in April and broke his middle finger in three places. 'It was a stupid thing to do,' he admitted. Yet it also forced him to take a much-needed rest from the game at a time when he was 'beginning to feel sick of tennis'.

The way he reached the final of the Stella Artois Championships two weeks before Wimbledon suggested that the enthusiasm – as well as the finger – was fully restored.

Croatia   Age: 26
World Ranking: 3

yevgeny KAFELNIKOV

Ever since losing in the first round a year earlier to Britain's Tim Henman, Kafelnikov had been determined to put things right by demonstrating that he can justify those who have tipped him for the highest honours in the game.

Although having learned his trade – and first made his mark – on clay, Kafelnikov's game is well suited to all surfaces. He is not only one of the most gifted but also one of the most durable players on the tour and in 1996, when he also collected his first Grand Slam tournament title at the French Open, he became the first player since John McEnroe to finish the year among the top five in singles and doubles.

After missing the 1996 US Open with a strained stomach muscle and the Australian Open due to a freak accident when he was training in a Melbourne gym on a punchbag, Kafelnikov lost his French title when he was beaten in the quarter-final by the brilliantly talented but unseeded eventual winner, Gustavo Kuerten from Brazil.

Yet victory on the grass in Halle, where 12 months earlier he had been runner-up, was his way of declaring his readiness to become the first Russian winner at The Championships.

| Russia   Age: 23 |
| World Ranking: 6 |

richard KRAJICEK

The 6ft 5in Dutchman, who uses his height, weight and power to full effect, was given so little chance of making an impact at Wimbledon in 1996 that it was only after Thomas Muster had withdrawn through injury that he was moved into a seeding position.

Not that he particularly minded. Indeed it was probably an added spur, for he went on to become the first player from Holland to win any Grand Slam singles title. His quarter-final match against Sampras was an epic and the only one in which he dropped sets.

Until then Krajicek's Wimbledon record had fallen well short of expectations, which is why the seeding committee originally overlooked him last time. And his post-Wimbledon form was also disappointing.

Yet since undergoing knee surgery at the end of the year, there were regular, though inconsistent, signs that, with his booming serve and ferocious groundstrokes, there would be no question of his easily relinquishing the Wimbledon crown which meant so much to him.

| Netherlands   Age: 25 |
| World Ranking: 5 |

michael CHANG

When Michael Chang first played at Wimbledon in 1988, at the age of 16, he performed with such scampering verve and vitality to win the first set from Henri Leconte and then force the exciting Frenchman to a tie-break in the second that it was felt that, as the years went by, even on grass he might overcome his lack of height and an in-built reluctance to play at the net.

Going into Wimbledon '97, however, that was still not the case. Although he reached the quarter-finals in 1994, that was his best effort in nine visits and, while he remains one of the quickest players on the tour and one of the most nimble-minded, he is too easily overpowered on this surface.

Chang, coached by his brother, has worked hard to improve his serve but his favourite tactic is still either to counter-punch or lure his opponent out of position so that he is ready to be passed.

He succeeds in this respect more often than most but not often enough to counter the current generation of huge servers who have also learned how to rally aggressively from the back.

USA   Age: 25
World Ranking: 2

thomas MUSTER

Somehow it seems Muster and Wimbledon are not destined to be bed-fellows. This was the second successive year that the Austrian had informed officials that he would not be playing after the draw had taken place.

In 1996, when he had shown that perhaps he need not fear grass courts after all by reaching the semi-finals at Queen's Club, even showing a willingness to serve and volley, the fittest player on the tour aggravated an old thigh muscle injury while playing in Halle.

This time, in a year when he had found the way to become a tournament winner on hard courts but lost his supremacy on clay, this first-round loser on each of his four visits to Wimbledon reported that he had injured his hip while playing in Rosmalen, so once again there was a vacant seeded place to be filled. It went to Sweden's Jonas Bjorkman.

Austria   Age: 29
World Ranking: 4

mark PHILIPPOUSSIS

There were some, not only Australians, who believed this could be the moment for the 6ft 4in right-hander to achieve a major breakthrough which would be as spectacular as his serve – at least until he drew Britain's Greg Rusedski in the first round. Then they were more reticent.

After a difficult time in 1996 trying to fulfil his obvious potential, Philippoussis had in recent months steadily matured in both his game and his temperament, with the two reaching perfection together as he beat Goran Ivanisevic for the Stella Artois title at Queen's Club, two weeks earlier.

Philippoussis likes to do most things in the fast lane. Nicknamed 'Scud' because of the record pace of his serves and driver of a flame-red 320 km/h Ferrari 355, he is regarded as the best Australian prospect since 1987 Wimbledon champion Pat Cash, one of the few players to win both the junior and main titles. Cash was junior champion in 1982. Phillippoussis was runner-up in 1994.

Australia   Age: 20
World Ranking: 13

boris BECKER

Boris Becker fell in love with Wimbledon even before he became the youngest champion when he won the title for the first time aged 17 in 1985. Yet in addition to his many highly emotional successes, there have been disasters, not least that moment a year earlier when a freak accident nearly ended his career.

Until that mishit return against Neville Godwin, which wrecked his right wrist, Becker had convinced himself that it was the year when a fourth Wimbledon title was within his grasp. He had won the Australian Open, his first Grand Slam tournament success for five years, in January and, more prohetically, won Queen's just as he had done in 1985.

Now, despite slipping to his lowest point for years in the world rankings, Becker, who had won at least one singles title on the tour for 12 consecutive years, realised this would be his last chance to win for that fourth time. The preparation was good, his game was good – but if it came down to five-setters, could he still stay the pace?

Germany   Age: 29
World Ranking: 18

martina HINGIS

The first six months of the year had seen Martina Hingis establish virtually unbroken supremacy in women's tennis, by a 16-year-old destined to become a mega-star since her mother, Melanie, named her after the first Martina (Navratilova) when she was born.

Although there was a time when Hingis was not sure whether to commit her talents wholly to tennis or horse-riding, there had not been too much doubt really since she became the youngest junior winner at a Grand Slam tournament at the French Open when she was 12.

Since then, records had fallen to her regularly and the way she won the Australian Open in January to become their youngest women's champion without dropping a set, overwhelming former champion Mary Pierce in the final, left few in doubt that over the next fortnight there could be more records to ring up.

Switzerland   Age: 16
World Ranking: 1

monica SELES

Over the years this most ferocious of hitters has often said that a player has to win Wimbledon before they can begin to be regarded as one of the all-time greats. That alone is a driving incentive to a player who has twice won the three other Grand Slam tournaments in the same year but missed out on the one which she feels matters most.

Whether it would have happened by now but for the horrific incident when she was stabbed on court in Hamburg in 1993 and out of tennis for three summers one will never know, but it is highly likely, for by then she had firmly taken over from Steffi Graf, who beat her in the 1992 final, as world number one.

In 1996, she won the first grass-court title of her career in the Direct Line Championships at Eastbourne but the Yugoslav-born American, double-handed on both flanks most of the time, lost to Katarina Studenikova of the Czech Republic in the second round of The Championships.

Although not naturally comfortable on grass, the accuracy and control, as well as the strength, of her shots, plus enormous determination, mean she always has a chance. This time, though, an emotional strain made it more difficult.

USA   Age: 23
World Ranking: 2

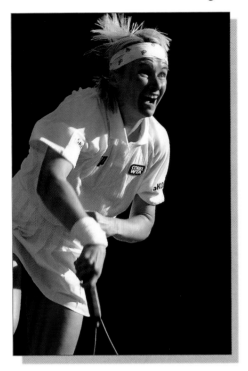

jana NOVOTNA

Until she wins Wimbledon, Jana Novotna will always be remembered as the girl who cried on the shoulder of the Duchess. It is little comfort to her that she has not yet done so despite a talent which should blossom more profitably than most on grass courts.

The one quality which Novotna, one of a dying breed of natural serve-and-volleyers in women's tennis, will never compromise is her determination to be aggressive at every opportunity. It is an engaging, often successful, strength, especially on grass and faster surfaces. It can also be a devastating weakness, as she knows only too well.

One of her problems is that she often creates for herself too many options, even within a rally, and then, at the most critical moment, chooses the wrong one. Wimbledon '97 seemed to offer the best chance of her winning the title if she could keep her game and nerve together. Experience, certainly, was on her side.

Czech Republic   Age: 28
World Ranking: 3

iva MAJOLI

A check of Iva Majoli's record at Wimbledon on the eve of the 1997 Championships hardly warranted a second glance. She was still seeking her first win either as a junior or main-draw player, in singles and doubles. 'It can only get better,' she joked when first drawing attention to the figures.

Things, though, were starting to be different now, as she had demonstrated a few weeks earlier when she not only joined the elite list of Grand Slam tournament winners at the French Open but also stopped Martina Hingis's unbeaten record for the year at 40.

Majoli, who played with such all-round class and all-court ability on that occasion, had then made it clear that, having put fun before her tennis as the top priority for most of her teenage years, she was ready to fight for the chance to win every title on all surfaces. How well she was to play this year, when victory celebrations after Paris and the weather gave her virtually no time to prepare on grass, would be worth noting for future reference.

Croatia   Age: 19
World Ranking: 4

lindsay DAVENPORT

The American is one of that all-too-large group of players who have so far failed to reach their potential, despite intermittent demonstrations that perhaps they are about to do so.

Among such occasions have been the way the big-hitting, amiable Californian won the gold medal at the Olympic Games in Atlanta and, also in 1996, beat Steffi Graf and Anke Huber in successive matches to win the first title of her career, in Los Angeles.

To date, though, despite having the serve, height and weight of shot to make at least a reasonable impact at Wimbledon, her best effort before this year was in reaching the quarter-finals in 1994.

An outstanding junior, Davenport, coached by Robert Van't Hof, who was also a leading junior player in his day, is conscious that she has to be careful to watch her weight, for lack of mobility has been one of her frailties often exposed by her opponents, especially in later rounds of tournaments.

USA   Age: 21

World Ranking: 8

amanda COETZER

The blonde South African may be one of the smallest players on the women's tour, at 5ft 2in, but she is one of the feistiest, as several of those above her in the rankings could testify.

While others may have inwardly welcomed the absence of Steffi Graf, through injury, at Wimbledon '97, Coetzer would have been more than happy if she had found herself in the same section of the draw as the German, for she beat her in the Monica Seles comeback tournament in Toronto in 1995 and in both this year's earlier Grand Slam tournaments in Australia and the French Open.

Coached by Australian fitness expert Gavin Hopper, who has encouraged this fighter, who was already as nippy as a whippet about the court, to place even greater emphasis on mental, as well as physical, stamina, Coetzer has the ability, and the will, to beat most on her day.

South Africa   Age: 25

World Ranking: 7

anke HUBER

7

It is hard to imagine that this talented and attractive player is still only 22 for it seems like an age since she first burst on the scene, with her imposing serve and solid groundstrokes, which prompted some fellow countrymen to dub her 'The new Steffi'.

Far from a help, it has been a burden. The best she can look back upon so far at Wimbledon is reaching the fourth round in 1991, when many felt it would be only a matter of time before she would be pressing seriously for top honours, and again in 1995, by which time reservations had already started to creep in.

On form, Huber is a splendid player to watch. She moves well and, although she could hardly be termed an enthusiastic volleyer, there is a handsome combination of strength and subtlety with which she loves to wear down opponents in rallies. Yet inconsistency, especially on her serve, which can then have a disastrous effect on confidence, remains a problem.

Germany   Age: 22

World Ranking: 10

arantxa SANCHEZ VICARIO

8

Although first coming to the fore on clay courts, this tenacious fighter has an impressively consistent record on all surfaces, which is a testimony to her commitment, her skill and, certainly in the case of Wimbledon, her determination to learn how to be a threat on grass – still apparently feared by so many Spaniards.

Three times winner of the French Open, she also won the US Open in 1994 and has been runner-up twice in both the other Grand Slam tournaments, in Australia and at Wimbledon, where she won the doubles in 1995.

Indeed at Wimbledon she was in the two previous finals, losing tough, exciting contests against Steffi Graf on both occasions. As a retriever, under pressure, Sanchez has few peers and her evident, enthusiastic enjoyment of winning a long, exhausting rally with a pass, or, just as likely, a drop shot, ensures that her tennis is never dull.

Spain   Age: 25

World Ranking: 6

A spectacular aerial view of Wimbledon during the height of The Championships – and the panoramic view of the new No. 1 Court enjoyed by some of its 11,000 spectators.

At a time when there were drought warnings in most parts of Britain, almost four inches of rain fell on London SW19 in the seven days leading into the 111th staging of The Championships. It was hardly the christening anyone had in mind for the unveiling of the magnificent new No. 1 Court which is the centrepiece of an ambitious long-term development plan designed to maintain Wimbledon's reputation as the world's most prestigious tournament into the 21st century.

The problems that caused, not to the well-protected court, of course, but to almost everyone else from spectators to players, were considerable. The downpours which had severely ravaged the qualifying events at Roehampton the week before had also taken their toll of something one normally takes for granted – the grass-covered car parks.

A limitation on spaces which could still be used, coupled with inevitable added security checks on cars and people after the catastrophic disruption of the Grand National race at Aintree a few months earlier, caused the sort of delays for some before they could take their place inside the grounds which will doubtless pass into family folklore.

The extra effort was well rewarded. Alan Mills, the tournament referee, had scheduled 69 matches on the day's programme. When failing light and an increasingly slippery surface brought a halt to the Centre Court thriller between Greg Rusedski and Mark Philippoussis, the only ones still playing after the third rain break of the day, only 19 had been completed. And three of those were doubles qualifying matches which, for the first time, were staged at the All England Club itself – refugees from Roehampton, where they should have ended four days earlier. Yet for all that there was an abundance of emotion, excitement and late-night drama.

The emotion came during the simple but colourful official opening ceremony for the 11,000-seat new No. 1 Court, performed by the President of the All

England Club, HRH the Duke of Kent. To mark the occasion, winners of three or more singles titles had been invited to take part. The ovation as, one by one, they appeared, grew as the spirit of the occasion was caught by a crowd many of whom were suddenly recalling their own great memories of matches they had seen these outstanding champions play: Louise Brough, Margaret Court, Rod Laver, Billie Jean King, as ebullient as ever, John Newcombe, Chris Evert, a suddenly greying John McEnroe, all smiles as never before on a Wimbledon court, Martina Navratilova, Boris Becker, resplendent in his dark business suit, and then Pete Sampras. There was due recognition too of Britain's three post-war lady champions sitting together watching the proceedings – Angela Mortimer, Ann Jones and 'the Kentish maid', as the master of ceremonies, John Barrett, called Virginia Wade.

One by one the three-times or more winners were presented to the Duke of Kent, who then performed the ceremonial ritual of measuring the net before declaring the new stadium open. It was time for play to begin. Alas, the rain decided otherwise. No sooner had British number one Tim Henman, proud to have been given the opportunity to be

Sir Geoffrey Cass, President of the Lawn Tennis Association, HRH the Duke of Kent, John Curry and Christopher Gorringe, respectively President, Chairman and Chief Executive of the All England Club, come to attention during the opening ceremony for the new No. 1 Court.
Below: John McEnroe, Boris Becker and Pete Sampras share a lighter moment.

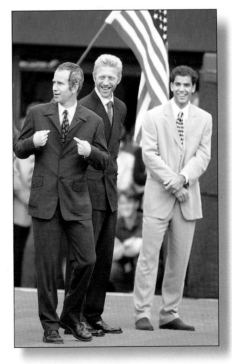

Above: Martina Navratilova shows her salver to the crowd as Chris Evert and John Curry join in the applause for the record nine-times ladies' singles champion.

Main photo: The colourful and happy scene during the parade by ten players who had won the singles title three times or more, as Rod Laver, regarded by many as the best of all time, receives his commemorative salver from the Duke of Kent.

the first winner on the new No. 1 Court, reached the final moments of his warm-up with Canada's Daniel Nestor than they were forced to take cover.

The ceremony meant that not only No. 1 Court but also the Centre Court broke from its traditional 2 p.m. start on the first day and was due to start at 2.15 p.m. instead. It was actually a few minutes after that when Richard Krajicek walked out to meet the little-known German, Marcello Craca, to maintain a tradition the defending champion had been looking forward to from almost the moment he had become the first Dutchman to win the title 12 months earlier. Krajicek and Craca did not even get so far as Henman and Nestor at the first attempt. They had only just walked out and placed their bags on the ground when they had to grab them again and hurry off. Not that Krajicek minded.

'The longer I hold on to the title, the better I like it,' he had said earlier, when first told that he would not be needed at '2 p.m. precisely'. As for waiting while a ceremony was taking place elsewhere, Krajicek said, 'These guys are legends. I saw Laver and Navratilova here and all the great champions. I think it's great they get such recognition. They are the people who built the game and are still the faces of the game. Some still play now and it's good that you cherish them. I applaud these kind of ceremonies.'

As for his own first-round performance, Krajicek, who made a few more unforced errors than he would have liked and was relieved to get through the first-set tie-break in which Craca, 1–3 down, recovered to have two serves for the set at 5–4, said, 'A day like this has a special tension. I was pretty happy when the match was finished.'

The day before Krajicek had won the tournament in Rosmalen, where the weather was also indifferent, but officials there had assured him and Wimbledon that if they could not finish on time then everyone was agreeable to the final being abandoned and the prize money divided. Krajicek had been saying for months

that nothing would prevent him from arriving at Wimbledon on time. Indeed to make sure, he had a helicopter waiting to fly him straight from Holland to land him on the roof of his Chelsea hotel.

Long before Krajicek or Henman were taking their places on the two main stages, some had already overcome their first hurdles – none happier than second-seeded Goran Ivanisevic, who had struck 24 aces and taken only 67 minutes to beat the Romanian, Dino Pesariu, 6–1, 6–3, 6–3. 'That was the perfect way for me to start the tournament,' said the Croatian, who was one of the few feeling grateful to the recent wet days. 'It's stopped me spending as much time on the practice court as usual and I feel a lot fresher,' he added. But the question his supporters were asking was 'Can the mood last?'

Another Day One tradition has also developed over the years. It is one of the all too few days when British players are most likely to win the main headlines. This time was no exception. Henman launched the new No. 1 Court in triumph at the start of the day and then Greg Rusedski provided enormous excitement by taking a two-sets lead, both in tie-breaks, over seventh-seeded Mark Philippoussis and had broken to lead 3–1 in the third when, at 8.49 p.m., failing light and an increasingly slippery court forced an overnight wait.

Everyone knew that there would be no place for faint hearts in this first meeting between the two fastest servers in the world. By the time they came off court, there had not just been 32 aces, 21 of them by the British left-hander, but both had delivered serves of 138 mph, the fastest recorded on the Centre Court since IBM timings began officially in 1992.

The overnight postponement, although inevitable, was an obvious disappointment to the enthusiastic crowd and even more so to Rusedski, who carried on where he left off when winning Nottingham and reaching a career-best world ranking of 27 – full of confidence. He did have some vital help from his opponent, though. Philippoussis had led

Richard Krajicek (opposite) took time to find the rhythm and command he wanted as he began the defence of his title against Germany's Marcello Craca.

Iva Majoli, the newly crowned French Open champion after becoming the first player in the year to beat Martina Hingis, was one of the few top-line women competitors in action on the day. It was with some trepidation that the 19-year-old Croatian stepped out on Court 2, with its notorious reputation for upsets, to face Argentinian Mariana Diaz-Oliva. Majoli, after all, had not hitherto won a match in singles, doubles or as a junior at Wimbledon.

No wonder that, after winning 2–6, 6–0, 6–3, she said, 'I'm almost as happy as when I won at Roland Garros.' She had been given plenty of advice. Peter Fleming, the former men's doubles champion, gave her tactical hints, Martina Navratilova reminded her to bend her knees and move well and Nick Bollettieri, whom she calls 'my second father', provided constant encouragement from the side of the court.

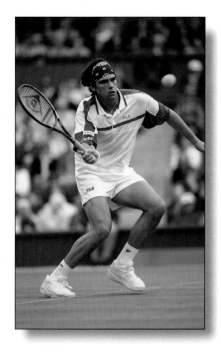

6–2 in the second-set tie-break but at 6–5, with nerves taking over, he double-faulted twice to go from holding a fourth set point to giving Rusedski his first. It was all that was needed. Then another double fault enabled the rampant Rusedski to break for 3–1, just three games away from what would be another memorable victory.

Henman's performance was less vibrant, especially in a tense first set, but at least the British number one, still struggling to justify his high profile after an elbow operation in March, showed the fortitude necessary when things might have turned against him. In a thrilling tie-break at the end of an erratic first set, Henman, whose serve had been wavering, saved three set points, two of them with aces, before going on, via a second rain break, to beat Nestor 7–6, 6–1, 6–4.

The next Henman opponent remained undecided. He had doubtless hoped that it would be Jamie Delgado, his schoolboy friend who in those days was the one in the spotlight. Delgado's hopes were fading like the light, however, for he was two sets to one and 2–5 down to the Frenchman, Jerome Golmard, when their match was halted.

Henman and Rusedski were not alone in raising British spirits. The day had started well for home followers when 6ft 7in Andrew Richardson justified the first wild card he had been offered in five years with a 7–6, 6–3, 6–3 defeat of Spanish qualifier Sergi Duran.

The Lincolnshire left-hander served well throughout but it was the growing strength of his returns which made it an increasingly encouraging performance by a late developer who credits Henman and Rusedski for providing him with an added incentive to do well. 'I struggled for a few years but I've grown up with Tim and it's easier having someone like him and Greg, who's been great as well, showing you how it can be done.'

British players earned the loudest cheers, especially Greg Rusedski (top right), who was on the verge of beating Mark Philippoussis (top left) when bad light stopped play. Above: Two other first-round British winners, Andrew Richardson (left) and Jamie Delgado. Right: Tim Henman became the first winner on the new No. 1 Court.

The victory salute from Greg Rusedski (left) after completing his victory over Mark Philippoussis but contrasting moods from Chris Wilkinson (right) in triumph and Pat Cash in defeat, as fans appreciate what the new No. 1 Court has to offer.

WIMBLEDON

day **2**

TUESDAY 24 JUNE

Smiles all round as Mark Petchey (right), Wayne Ferreira (below left), Karen Cross, the first British player to win through the qualifying for the ladies' singles since 1976, and Martin Lee progress to the second round.

For the second successive year, Day Two belonged to the Brits. A year earlier, Tim Henman had made the major news and featured on all the television bulletins by beating Yevgeny Kafelnikov. This time, when a record second-day crowd of 37,871 enjoyed a day of uninterrupted tennis, it was Greg Rusedski, tenaciously finishing off a superb first-round victory over Mark Philippoussis, and Chris Wilkinson, recovering from two sets down to beat another seed, Jonas Björkman, who took pride of place.

What made the day even more uplifting for British supporters, though, was that it did not end there. Late in the evening, Mark Petchey on Court 18 and Martin Lee, even more encouragingly, on Court 13 also played above themselves to make sure there would be at least six British men in the second round. In addition, Karen Cross, who had needed a wild card just to get into the qualifying competition, produced a performance which belied her world ranking of 322 to upset the vastly more experienced American, Linda Harvey Wild.

Rusedski took only 14 heavy-serving minutes to complete his resounding 7–6, 7–6, 6–3 victory over the seventh-seeded Philippoussis but every one of them was cherished by all but the brave flag-waving Australians in the Centre Court crowd.

'If Greg can serve like that in other matches who knows how far he can go?' was the prophetic observation from his well-beaten opponent, who had thought he was ready to do well at The Championships this year. 'That's definitely the highest level of serving which anyone has sustained over such a long period against me.'

Most of the work, of course, had been done the night before. And that is when Philippoussis also inflicted too much damage on himself with those double faults – two more in this last act for a total of 13. 'Losing that second set from 6–2 was really where the match was lost for me,' he said, no doubt also haunted at that moment by the memory of how he had lost the junior boys' final three years earlier because of too many double

faults. Yet, as Wayne Ferreira, the 15th-seeded South African, was proving at the same time against another Australian, Scott Draper, even a two-sets lead in a match delayed overnight need not necessarily be a lost cause. In his first match since being forced to default to Petr Korda at the French Open after twisting his ankle while practising, Ferreira made the new day a completely new match by storming back to win 6–7, 3–6, 6–4, 6–0, 7–5.

For Philippoussis to have had any chance of staging a similar recovery, he would have needed to break back straight away. Rusedski, who admitted he had found it difficult to sleep the night before as he kept thinking of how the match still had to be won, made sure there was no let-up on his part. In the first game when they resumed, he held for 4–1 with three more blistering serves and the first of five more aces, the last of them on match point, taking his total for the match to 27.

Serving for victory, Rusedski hit such a great serve when he was 15–30 that he used the same ball for the next point. And when that was a 'let' he called for it back rather than use another he was offered. 'It was just a lucky ball, I guess. It won me three straight points so it must have been doing all right.'

He also carried what he called 'another lucky charm' – a piece of paper with the names of a group of children from Great Ormond Street Hospital belonging to the Andrea Jaeger Tennis Foundation, which caters specifically for youngsters with illnesses likely to be terminal. 'They wanted to have their picture taken with me and then asked for my autograph,' said Rusedski. 'I only thought it was fair that I then asked them for theirs.'

Chris Wilkinson thought his luck was out when the withdrawal of Thomas Muster, the sixth seed, meant a change of first-round opponent and he instead found himself facing Bjorkman, now the 17th seed and ranked almost 200 places above him. Wilkinson, who had won at

least one match at Wimbledon in his five previous years, had fancied his chances of beating the Austrian, who in four visits had not won a single match. Bjorkman, he felt, might be a different proposition. One of the best returners in the game, he had only recently beaten Pete Sampras on grass at Queen's Club.

'To be honest I didn't really fancy my chances against him,' said Wilkinson. Yet he shrugged off the disappointment just as determinedly as he fought back from trailing by two sets to one for by far his best Wimbledon victory, 7–6, 0–6, 5–7, 6–3, 6–4.

His tenacity was ultimately the key as he beat the Swede, who had also fallen to a British player, Luke Milligan, in the first round a year earlier. The greatest test of Wilkinson's character came when he held for 3–3 in the final set in a sixth game which lasted 13 minutes – only six minutes shorter than the second set he had just lost when play was stopped the night before – and during which he saved eight break points.

In a match of many rallies, Bjorkman seemed so dismayed at losing those chances that he then lost his service in the seventh game and the semi-finalist at both Queen's Club and Rosmalen in his build-up to Wimbledon merely said, 'It can't be much worse than it was today.'

Wilkinson, meanwhile, was rightly elated. Reflecting on the drama of that final set, he said, 'At that stage technique goes out of the window. It takes courage. But it's easier if you're English. The crowd gets behind you and I love the atmosphere here.'

Martin Lee, who this time last year was struggling to cope with the pressures of being ranked number one among world juniors, was clearly happy to be free from such mental shackles as he returned magnificently and eventually served just as effectively to win the first match he had played in a Grand Slam tournament. Portugal's 120-ranked Nuno Marques, who had lost in the first round in both of his previous visits, may not have been the most notable scalp but

it was a significant psychological boost for the 19-year-old Worthing left-hander, who won 7–5, 6–3, 6–3.

'At first I was really nervous and it was only my returns which kept me in the first set,' he said. 'But the more returns I hit [and it was one of the best which carried him to match point], the more my confidence returned to my serve.'

Mark Petchey's 6–1, 6–2, 6–1 defeat of the Slovakian, Jan Kroslak, was a pleasant surprise for more than one reason. Although Kroslak was hampered to some extent by a knee injury, Petchey had not previously won a match on the senior tour this year and to compound his problems had been suffering from a temperature and sore throat for four days.

Cross, the first British woman to emerge from the qualifying competition since fellow Devonian Corinne Molesworth reached the third round before losing to Evonne Goolagong in 1976, could hardly contain her delight when Wild netted a routine forehand to confirm her 6–4, 6–2 victory.

Having played at Wimbledon three times before and then won three matches in the qualifying tournament, Cross did not appear at all nervous. She started well, immediately broke her opponent's serve and, as she put it, 'just kept going. I feel I'm in the second round on merit.'

Other British ladies were not so successful, particularly Clare Wood, who, while thrilled to be making her final appearance at The Championships on Centre Court, was given no chance to do more than strike a few stylish winners as Arantxa Sanchez Vicario, delighted to have been chosen to open Ladies' Day in place of the absent Steffi Graf, romped through 6–0, 6–0.

Chris Wilkinson (left) was often at full stretch but he responded brilliantly to the challenge by beating the seeded Jonas Bjorkman from two sets down.

No respite for Clare Wood (bottom) as Arantxa Sanchez Vicario (below) trounced her 6–0, 6–0.

Altogether six seeds were beaten. Apart from Bjorkman and Philippoussis, Gustavo Kuerten, the new French Open champion, and Michael Chang departed the men's singles. Kuerten was beaten 6–3, 6–4, 4–6, 1–6, 6–4 by Justin Gimelstob, the powerfully built young American prospect. Yet Kuerten,

crowding him effectively at the net, had looked well in command. But for a couple of missed volleys in the tenth game of the final set, the personable Kuerten might have graduated at least into the second round.

Apart from the brief excitement when Rusedski was winning, the Centre Court had to wait until fifth-seeded Chang met Todd Woodbridge, the right-handed member of the awesome Australian doubles team with Mark Woodforde, for a match to get their teeth into. They had admired Sanchez's brief demolition of Wood and an overwhelming 6–1, 6–1 victory for the almost unbelievably mature Anna Kournikova, just 16, against Chanda Rubin.

Chang v. Woodbridge was their match of the day, though. It lasted four hours and in a thrilling final set Woodbridge led 5–1 but Chang, desperate to avoid a first-round defeat for the second successive year, struck back, helped by his opponent's errors and tension, to lead 6–5 before going down 7–6, 3–6, 6–2, 3–6, 8–6.

In the ladies' singles, where top-seeded Martina Hingis was stretched harder than had been expected before beating 218th-ranked Anne Kremer, Luxembourg's only representative in the draw, 6–4, 6–4, Kimberley Po, seeded 13, was beaten 3–6, 7–5, 6–2 by Kerry-Ann Guse and 15th seed Ruxandra Dragomir, who lost 5–7, 6–2, 10–8 to Germany's Andrea Glass, bade farewell for another year.

No worries for the leading men. Pete Sampras, once he settled down, lifted his game impressively from 3–4 in the first set to beat Mikael Tillstrom 6–4, 6–4, 6–2, Boris Becker sailed past the Spaniard, Marcos Gorriz, at 33 the oldest player in the draw, also in straight sets, Michael Stich, another former German champion, enjoyed the start of his retirement Wimbledon by beating Jim Courier 7–6, 7–5, 7–6 and Yevgeny Kafelnikov dropped only six games against Spaniard Juan-Antonio Marin.

A busy, eventful day.

First-round defeats for French champions, past and present. Below: Brazil's Gustavo Kuerten puts on a brave face as he loses to Justin Gimelstob. Left: Jim Courier is philosophical in defeat by Michael Stich.

seeded 14, could take heart from a match in which he said he had 'come to learn for the future'. He did so quickly enough to draw level after Gimelstob,

Overleaf: Not even Michael Chang's explosive energy was enough to thwart unseeded Australian Todd Woodbridge.

WIMBLEDON

day **3**

WEDNESDAY 25 JUNE

THE CHAMPIONSHIPS

An aptly decorated umbrella provides a humorous touch in front of the giant screen by No. 1 Court, showing a re-run of the opening day's presentation ceremony to try and take everyone's minds off the weather. It was not easy. A cushion seller (above) kept herself well wrapped up but the rain did not daunt the enthusiasm of Tim Henman fans (above right), even though the courts had to be covered and remained that way most of the day.

Jana Novotna (below) was one of the lucky ones on Day Three, inasmuch as her shaky win over Wiltrud Probst was one of only two matches to finish. The other featured Monica Seles (opposite), but even that was delayed for 30 minutes immediately after Rachel McQuillan had saved the former world champion's first match point.

The weather did its worst. Not a single ball was struck until 6.04 p.m. on the Centre Court clock, and although Monica Seles then rapidly powered her way to victory in a first-round match which originally figured on Monday's Order of Play the rain nearly thwarted her again.

Seles was leading the 105th-ranked Australian, Rachel McQuillan, by a set and 5–2 and had reached match point when up went the umbrellas again. That infuriating drizzle, which had been the main reason for the day's frustrating delays, had returned. They played the match point but after McQuillan had saved it with a high volley as Seles produced more of a defensive return than an attempted match-winning pass, the American was the one who wanted to stop even before it would have been inevitable anyway.

When they returned after another 30 minutes in a locker room which must have started to feel like a prison during the hours of waiting, Seles had to wait just one minute 43 seconds and play only four more points, the last of them appropriately enough being another of her fiercely driven crosscourt returns, to be safely into round two.

The former world number one wrapped up the first set in 18 minutes and had taken eleven consecutive points to reach 3–0 in the second before McQuillan won her first game and acknowledged the cheers of what, despite the four hours' wait before they had seen any play at all, was still an almost full Centre Court crowd with a huge grin and an arms-aloft salute.

Seles went on to win 6–0, 6–2 and was relieved that her decision to ask for play to be suspended, rather than see if

another two points would have been enough, did not backfire. 'I was debating if I should do that after I lost the first match point,' she said. 'But it was so slippery that I didn't think it was worth the risk. I'm only pleased we could finish it today and not have to wait overnight.'

Asked what it had been like waiting for so long to start the match, Seles said, 'It was tough. I was supposed to play on Monday so I was here all day then. Then I was expecting to play yesterday. But it's been tough on all the players. I'm one of the lucky ones. I've finished tonight.'

Amid that pleasure, however, there was obvious sadness as Seles talked in the interview room about how difficult it also was for her to be at Wimbledon this year without the ever-present support of her father and coach, Karoly. He was back home in Florida undergoing treatment for stomach cancer. 'I'm going through a tough stage right now,' she said. 'Things go on in your life which are much bigger than this tournament.'

Indeed. Although there was eventually play on 14 other courts as well, except on No. 1 Court none of the matches went beyond two games. Elena Likhovtseva and Natasha Zvereva followed Seles and McQuillan on to Centre Court and Likhovtseva had time to establish a 6–2, 4–0 lead before play was abandoned for the day. The only other match which actually finished was that on No. 1 Court, where Jana Novotna, despite torturing herself and her followers by losing control in the second set, beat the 28-year-old German, Wiltrud Probst, 6–4, 4–6, 6–0.

Novotna's main problem was that her serve started to let her down, a sure sign of nerves. On the other hand, she rallied so strongly, dropping only five points in a final set lasting a mere 17 minutes, that at least she left feeling content.

That was hardly so in the case of tournament referee Alan Mills. He and his staff already faced a backlog of 40 matches when they were planning the day's programme. Now that total had reached three figures and they were hardly comforted by the news that not only was this already the wettest June since 1991, when not all first-round matches had been completed by the first Friday night, but that the forecast for the next few days was anything but encouraging.

Officials were understandably playing down at that stage the assumption that there would have to be another 'People's Sunday', like the one in 1991, when admission on the middle Sunday was a cut-price £10 a head and around 25,000 flocked into the grounds for what became one of the most memorable days in Wimbledon history. That, everyone agreed, should only be the last resort.

The patience and tolerance, at least among the majority, of Wimbledon crowds never ceases to amaze visitors from abroad. More than 10,000 were queuing in the rain, many having been there all night, when the gates opened on a day when everyone sensed there was a real danger of Wimbledon suffering what would have been only its tenth completely blank day in half a century. Hundreds more queued outside even after the gates were initially closed because the grounds were full. Forecasts of brief dry spells from the weather forecasters came and went several times during the day.

'They're the people I feel sorry for,' said Alan Mills, looking out of his office late in the afternoon, when he was already sending players home and reorganising Thursday's programme to begin early on all courts. 'They've been here for hours just waiting and hoping to see some play. For some of them, no doubt, it's the only time they will be here. We're doing our best to get matches played but at the same time we have to make sure that when they do begin the courts aren't dangerous.'

It was just about then that the most recent weather forecast suggested there was even the risk of heavier rain. But this time it was the pessimistic rather than the optimistic view that was wrong. And while not much comfort to those waiting to see more than just a few minutes of tennis on the outside courts, at least for those on Centre and No. 1 Courts, some play was better than none.

WIMBLEDON

days **4&5**

THURSDAY 26 JUNE
& FRIDAY 27 JUNE

As if the previous day had not been bad enough, Day Four was infinitely worse. Although it had just about been dry enough for the practice courts at Aorangi to be used by a lucky few for 20 minutes, it was drizzling by 10 a.m. and by 11 a.m., when play should have started – an hour earlier than normal – on the outside courts, it was raining steadily.

Over the next seven hours until play was abandoned for the day at 6 p.m., the only change was whether it was raining lightly, steadily or coming down in torrents. As usual some of the Service Stewards came to the fore, choreographing spectators in the stands in various forms of entertainment such as sing-a-longs, the Conga and even just throwing tennis balls to each other.

The cruel reality, though, was that it was a waste for all concerned, albeit only the fifth time in 25 years that a day had passed without at least some play. Alan Mills, the referee, described it as 'the wettest day I can remember' in terms of the sheer volume of water involved. Even so there was still an obvious reluctance to commit to play on the middle Sunday as a means of making up for lost time.

Mr Mills was still trying to put a brave face on things, pointing out that even in 1991, when the weather in the first four days of the first week had been even worse, allowing only 52 matches to be played, compared with 96 this time, the tournament still finished on time. In that year, however, the weather relented by the first Friday – and there was also that memorable middle Sunday, which Mr Mills called 'the most inspiring day in all my time at Wimbledon'.

This time the forecast gave little hope of an immediate improvement so, as officials pointed out, the weather prospects would be an additional major factor as to whether play on the middle Sunday, while obviously an option, would even be worthwhile.

One time-saving measure had been announced. The men's doubles, at least through to the quarter-finals, was reduced to best of three sets, and although

it had never been done before Mr Mills agreed that the possibility of reducing one or more complete rounds of matches in the men's singles from five sets to three might also be something they should consider.

Almost inevitably, what Tim Phillips, chairman of the Order of Play Sub-Committee, called 'that hoary old chestnut' – whether or not the All England Club should have put a roof on the new No. 1 Court, so that at least there would have been some play for the paying fans – was brought out of the media cupboard.

The situation, as Mr Phillips explained, was the same as it had been when a roof for the Centre Court had been considered and rejected. A roof in itself would not satisfy every factor which had to be taken into account, such as that Wimbledon is an outdoor tournament; the vast majority of the players, as they had made clear in Australia, where there is a roof on the centre court, are against the idea; and providing tennis for one set of spectators on one court but not the others would only alienate even more, including the 10,000 or more who daily queued outside, many of them overnight.

As Mr Mills pointed out, while a grass court might not suffer from being covered for a few hours, for it to be covered and played on relentlessly for at least two days, which would have been the case this year, would probably render it unplayable for the rest of the tournament.

As everyone wended their way home after Day Four, it was still raining . . . Day Five, almost unbelievably, was more of the same. For only the second time in the history of The Championships and the first time since 1909, two consecutive days had been washed out. The only comforting thought for British supporters was that at least in 1909 there had been a British champion, Arthur W. Gore, the last British winner before Fred Perry, 25 years later.

There was nothing one could do as the weather refused to relent, except wait and hope to catch a glimpse of Tim Henman or the Williams sisters, Serena (left) and Venus, who found the delays just as frustrating as everyone else.

Overleaf: Raindrops were falling on the gates of the All England Club as well as on disappointed spectators.

WIMBLEDON

day**6**

SATURDAY 28 JUNE

'So there really is a tennis court under those covers after all!' was one of the first comments overheard in the media room when the rain which had still been falling at 11 a.m., when matches on the outside courts should have started, finally stopped and, for the first time in three days, the covers came off.

It heralded the start of what was to become another of those extraordinarily memorable days for a whole variety of reasons, not least that after those two blank days 70 matches were completed, twenty more than referee Alan Mills had hoped for – and another eight were on court when the race to beat the rapidly fading light had to stop.

Suddenly, after a delay spanning 65 hours, there was action and excitement in all directions and the venomous black clouds which seemed to be heading towards the grounds at various stages of the afternoon for once veered clear of the All England Club. Two more men's seeds, most notably second favourite Goran Ivanisevic, were knocked out, while the Wimbledon debut of Venus Williams, just 17, complete with her beaded hair, half of them in the All England Club colours, ended with her surprise first-round defeat by Magdalena Grzybowska, one of two Polish players in the draw.

The defeat of Ivanisevic, twice a runner-up, was a huge shock and disappointment, especially to his large and devoted contingent of female supporters. He served 46 aces, breaking the record for one match at The Championships of 42 set by Britain's John Feaver against John Newcombe in 1976. He too lost.

Ivanisevic was beaten 6–3, 2–6, 7–6, 4–6, 14–12 on Court 3 by Sweden's Magnus Norman, who had celebrated his 21st birthday three weeks earlier at

Venus Williams (previous pages), resplendent with her beaded hairstyle, was one of the most publicised newcomers at The Championships this year.

Opposite: Magnus Norman recovered from a racing heartbeat to upset second-seeded Goran Ivanisevic, who again paid a heavy price for missed opportunities.

While even some leading politicians were starting to take issue with the British tabloid newspapers for spending so much space in words and pictures on how some of the most attractive players in the ladies' singles looked, rather than played, Martina Hingis came to the defence of the media.

The top seed, having changed the shirt and shorts she wore in her first match for something not quite so revealing for her second-round meeting with Olga Barabanschikova, said, 'I'm always good for advice. It wasn't great, the last dress and the shorts were pretty short', she acknowledged. 'The pictures were a help.'

the French Open by defeating Pete Sampras. The Croatian left-hander was so angry that he refused to attend a media conference and was later fined £1,300, the statutory figure on the men's tour. Ivanisevic, who had twice saved match points, had four times been one point from breaking through in the fifth set.

What made his defeat all the more extraordinary was that at 6–6 in the final set Norman needed treatment for chest pains, thought to be associated with the irregular heartbeat problem which in the past has occasionally forced him to default or not play matches.

This time the problem passed off swiftly so that he was able to continue with his fine volleying, and generally tidier game, until a bullet serve down the middle – which Ivanisevic felt looked long – in the 23rd game proved to be

worth more than one point psychologically. For although he continued to hit a few good blows, that was the moment when the second seed's body language indicated that he felt it was a lost cause.

Spain's Carlos Moya, who suffered a not unexpected second-round defeat at the hands of the ever-reliable American, Richey Reneberg, was the only other seed to fall on the day, although two of them had frights. Wayne Ferreira was pushed to 9–7 in the final set by Frenchman Rodolphe Gilbert, and Richard Krajicek was a set and a break down against Andrei Pavel before his serve slotted into place and carried him to success, also in the fifth.

Sunday morning headlines, though, were mainly provided by British players, led by Tim Henman, Greg Rusedski, Andrew Richardson and Karen Cross.

During practice that morning, Rusedski had slipped and suffered a slight pull in his back. The injury continued to haunt him on court, until he became a joyous jumping jack as he finally beat the American, Jonathan Stark, 4–6, 6–7, 6–4, 6–3, 11–9 in a match which was as thrilling as it was compelling for more than three hours.

For the first two sets, the anguish in Rusedski's mind, as much as his muscles, was clear. There were many missed serves between the flow of aces from both men, too many snatched volleys and, worst of all, the British player went two sets down after a tie-break in which he had three set points, two on serve, losing it 11–9 on his third double fault in the 20-point game.

Rusedski had never before won a match from two sets down. The road to recovery began with an immediate break in the third set but it was the tension of the fifth set which will be best remembered. At 2–2, Rusedski went to 30–40 on a sideline call which even Stefan Edberg might have questioned with more than a quizzical lifting of the eyebrows. Rusedski survived that moment but still lost the game – and his temper.

He raged at the umpire and, when

Greg Rusedski urges himself on to even greater effort, as girlfriend Lucy Connor (above left) shares the anxiety before his game came together well enough for him to beat the American, Jonathan Stark (below), who had held a two-sets lead.

Danny Sapsford (below) finally completed his defeat of Nicolas Perreira, while Karen Cross advanced to the third round.

Intense concentration from Anna Kournikova (opposite) shows why she has become such an exciting prospect. Grit and determination also greatly helped Magdalena Grzybowska to her surprise defeat of Venus Williams.

serving again two games later, emphasised his inner fury over that, and because he felt Stark was stalling, by slipping in an underarm serve which went wide. His cause looked hopeless. And yet, urged on by the crowd, at 4–5 in the fifth, when Stark was serving for the match, Rusedski produced a quartet of the most glorious returns just when they were most needed to make it 5–5. Although another ten games were necessary to bring him success, there was no stopping Rusedski then.

Jerome Golmard, a left-hander who was once a trainee carpenter and had shown that he knew his way around a grass court well enough by reaching the quarter-finals at Queen's Club, was Henman's second-round foe. The crucial moment was the first-set tie-break. Henman came from 2–4 to take it and thereafter his game broadened and strengthened as he completed a 7–6, 6–3, 6–3 victory.

Early-morning success for Danny Sapsford, as he completed a worthy victory over the former Wimbledon junior champion, Nicolas Perreira, in a match which had spanned four days, was short-lived for within a couple of hours, as everyone had to make concessions to help the tournament break into the backlog of matches, he was being beaten 6–2, 7–5, 6–2 by the Zimbabwean, Byron Black.

Sapsford's first-round victory made him one of seven British players who reached the second round – the same as in 1996 and again equalling the best figure since Open tennis, the merging of amateur and professional players in the same tournaments, was

first allowed in 1968. Andrew Richardson joined Henman and Rusedski in round three with a 6–3, 3–6, 6–4, 2–6, 6–2 defeat of Spaniard Juan Albert Viloca which took a good deal of dogged determination and heavy serving on his part, while Mark Petchey was encouragingly poised at 7–6, 3–3 against one of Germany's brightest prospects, Tommy Haas, when bad light stopped play for the day.

That, though, came too late for Chris Wilkinson, who, in rapidly decreasing light on Court 18, lost a two-sets lead to Mark Woodforde and went out in five to the Australian, while Martin Lee, who had sent British fans scurrying to his court when he took the first set, could not sustain the effort and was beaten 4–6, 6–2, 6–3, 6–4 by Frenchman Andrei Clement.

British ladies were also able to go home that evening smiling for a change. Not only had Karen Cross become the first British player to reach the third round since Anne Hobbs, seven years earlier, but Lorna Woodroffe's delayed first-round victory over 33rd-ranked Patty Schnyder, 18, from Switzerland meant she also still had a chance to do so. Cross beat Sanchez 6–4, 6–0, playing quite delightfully, but it was not quite the triumph some people imagined when they were looking at the scoreboards alongside the Debenture Holders' lounge. 'Wow, that Devon girl has knocked out Sanchez,' I heard someone say before she looked again and in a somewhat crestfallen way added to her friends, 'Oh sorry, it's not Arantxa but the other one,' whose name she could not remember. It was, of course, Maria-Antonia Sanchez Lorenzo, too long to fit fully on almost any results board.

Seldom has there been so much hype before a first appearance of a player at Wimbledon as that which preceded the arrival of Venus Williams. The student from Florida arrived on No. 1 Court with several swirls of the beads but in less than two hours the tall, striding teenager was departing again, beaten by an opponent whom the vast majority had not even heard of before she produced easily the biggest surprise of the first round.

Williams is spectacular to watch. She strikes the ball with considerable power on both flanks and covers the court well but, almost inevitably for someone with such limited competitive experience as a junior, she is short of strategy under pressure. That was clearly exposed as Grzybowska, 18, ranked 91 and so 32 places below the American, played with sufficient grit, purpose and occasional brilliance to win 4–6, 6–2, 6–4.

Twice in the final set Williams missed break points but she accepted her defeat philosophically, saying, 'I'm not too disappointed. It's my first Wimbledon and there will be many more to come.'

Anna Kournikova, another in the quartet of outstandingly talented teenagers attracting so much attention this year, looked likely to join Williams in defeat until she demonstrated enormous fighting spirit by recovering from a set and 1–5 down to upset the far more experienced German, Barbara Ritner, in a second-round encounter, 4–6, 7–6, 6–3. No such problems for Martina Hingis, a year younger than Williams, incidentally, or Iva Majoli, the new French Open champion, aged 19. They both advanced in comfort.

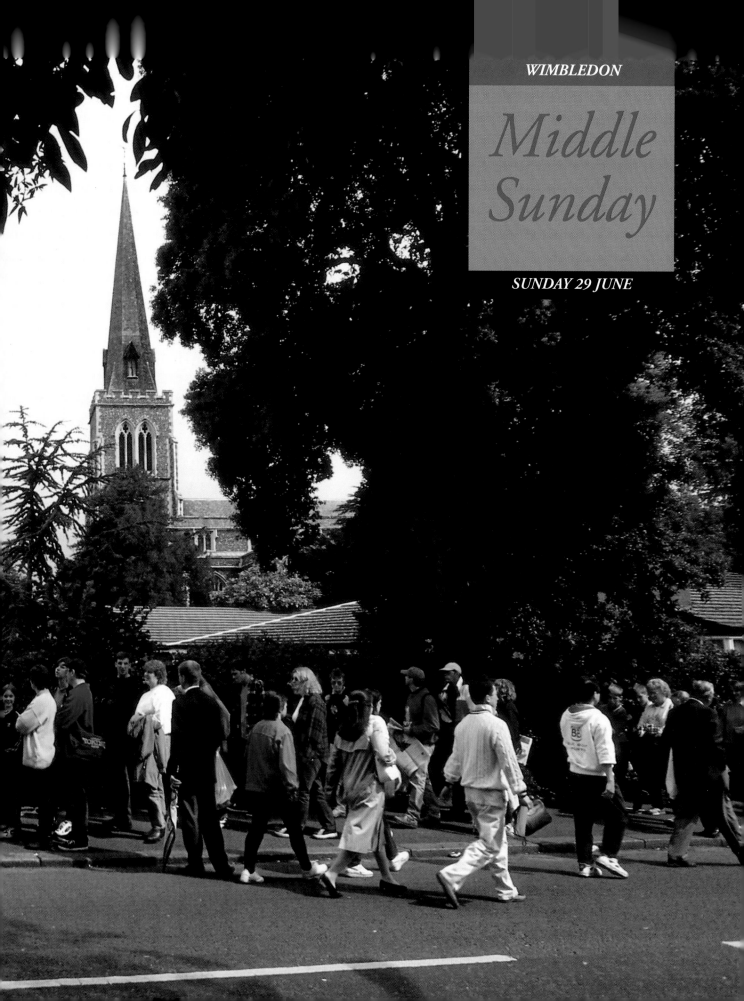

WIMBLEDON

Middle Sunday

SUNDAY 29 JUNE

For two days, at least, as the rain had poured down while first-round matches were still waiting to be played, there was the growing belief that play on the middle Sunday would become inevitable. The only time it had happened before was in 1991 when 'People's Day', as it became known, took its place in Wimbledon legend.

On that occasion, nearly 25,000 spectators – 24,894 to be precise – poured into the grounds despite the short notice (for the organisers as well as the crowds), creating an exhilarating atmosphere.

Some doubted whether the success of what at the time was supposed to be a one-off special occasion could be repeated. They need not have worried. The 1997 version surpassed the original both in terms of numbers and euphoria.

It was 4 p.m. on Saturday when confirmation came that there would be Sunday play. By then the queue for Monday had already begun – so that then became the queue for Sunday. By the time the gates opened at 10 a.m., it was estimated that one queue snaking its way round Wimbledon Park was two miles long. The other, heading towards and then past Wimbledon Park Station, was one and a half miles long.

The reduced ground capacity of 29,000 was reached at 2.35 p.m. but after consultation with the police and the Club Safety Officer another 3,000 were allowed in, with Members' and Debenture Holders' seats not needed on Centre Court being filled so that no one was disapppointed. There was little doubt who most of them most wanted to see: Tim Henman. Some had the name Tim painted on their faces. Others painted their faces with the Union flag, which was widely evident.

On a day when Greg Rusedski was to move through with predictable ease against fellow British left-hander Andrew Richardson, Henman's effort overshadowed everything else, including a 6–4, 6–3, 6–3 defeat for 15th seed Wayne Ferreira by Cedric Pioline, who, without focus or fanfare, was beginning

It was a long, tiring wait, especially for those who had queued overnight for play on Middle Sunday, but well worth it judging by the smiles of those who came patriotically dressed for the occasion – and by the hundreds without Centre Court seats who camped on the picnic lawns to share the excitement via the huge television screen as Tim Henman beat Paul Haarhuis.

Such was the interest among BBC Television viewers watching the Tim Henman–Paul Haarhuis contest that the audience reached a peak of 12.8m, 3m more than the best during the Richard Krajicek–MaliVai Washington final the year before and the best since 13.6m for Andre Agassi v. Goran Ivanisevic in 1992. To allow the match to be shown to the finish, the early evening news was delayed 40 minutes. So too was the programme which followed that – Songs of Praise, which had been recorded earlier on the new No. 1 Court.

The strain begins to show as Paul Haarhuis slips to defeat. Having double-faulted on a match point, the Dutchman eventually lost a titanic struggle against a triumphant Tim Henman (right).

Hen-man, Hen-man echoed round the arena and it continued to do so frequently throughout what became an epic match before reaching its frantic climax at 6.14 p.m., when the 22-year-old Oxfordshire player completed his triumph.

After three hours and 58 minutes of compelling play, 16 increasingly dramatic games since Haarhuis had double-faulted on a match point and two games since he had served his way out of a match point against him, Henman turned the most famous tennis arena in the world into a cauldron of cheering, flag-waving celebration with a perfect match-winning pass.

Henman won 6–7, 6–3, 6–2, 4–6, 14–12 on this day when Wembley came to Wimbledon and everyone enjoyed the partnership. 'From the word go the atmosphere created by the crowd was something I'd never experienced before,' said Henman after a match in which both players were as perilously close to losing as they were tantalisingly near to winning. 'I remember some of the feelings from a year ago when I beat [Yevgeny] Kafelnikov but this was at a totally different level,' Henman added, as he recalled his 1996 first-round victory over the sixth-seeded Russian. 'I've never played at Wembley but the crowd played a huge part in this match and that's as good as it gets in tennis.'

Although there were times when Cambridge-based Swiss umpire Andreas Egli had to work hard to keep the spectators' enthusiasm within bounds, Haarhuis never allowed himself to be rattled by the crowd's noisy, patriotic fervour for his opponent. After all, this was all quite friendly compared with the baying, far more intimidating New York night crowd he had faced when beating John McEnroe at the US Open in 1989.

It was much more a classic contest than classic tennis. But that hardly mattered and was only to be expected. Six times Henman looked poised to win the first set, thrice at 5–3 and then at 6–3 in the tie-break. Every chance was lost, three on double faults, before 63rd-

to produce the form which was to assume much more exciting significance in the days ahead.

When the British number one walked out with Dutchman Paul Haarhuis to begin their second-round contest, they were greeted with a Mexican wave and then the chanting started. The cry of ranked Haarhuis won it on his second set point.

Over the next two sets, Henman was in command. His first serve was working more fluently and he was opening up the court to put away winners with increasing zeal. Yet just when it looked as if he would sail on, one careless game in the third game of the fourth set, after he had missed two break points one game earlier, plunged the crowd into considerable anxiety.

In the thrilling final set, lasting 91 minutes, break points came and went for both players even before Haarhuis not only double-faulted on his match point but did so again on the next point to give Henman the chance to break back and earn another standing ovation. From 5–5 the match went with serve until Henman, who came within two points of victory at 8–7 and 12–11, reached a 13–12 lead.

At last Haarhuis, 31, one of the best doubles players in the world, cracked under the pressure of the Henman returns. With Haarhuis serving at 0–40, the crowd settled. So did Henman. The forehand return swept past Haarhuis. There was an eruption of cheers, not only within Centre Court but outside on the picnic lawns where thousands more, as they had done the day before, were following every point on a huge television screen.

Watching proudly from the players' box, alongside Henman's family and coach David Felgate, was Bill Knight, the former manager of men's tennis for the Lawn Tennis Association, who had been instrumental in steering the British hero in the right direction as a 17-year-old. Just as significantly on this chilly but heart-warming day for British tennis, when four players had places in the third round, was the memory that Knight, together with Mike Sangster, Tony Pickard and Keith Wooldridge, had formed the last domestic quartet to do so well, in 1964.

Rusedski, who had stolen all the headlines the day before with his fabulous comeback from two sets down against Jonathan Stark, returned to

Yevgeny Kafelnikov at full stretch on serve on his way to beating Spain's Javier Sanchez for a place in the third round.

Right: A defiant double-handed backhand return from left-hander Marcelo Rios, who had to work hard to fend off a resilient challenge from Holland's Dennis Van Scheppingen.

Conchita Martinez (opposite), the only former champion in the ladies' singles, saw her hopes of a repeat triumph vanish when she was beaten by Helena Sukova (below), whose doubles successes at The Championships meant she was far more at home on the testing grass-court surface.

Court 1 where his experience and power brought him a comfortable 6–3, 6–4, 6–4 victory over Richardson. The 6ft 5in Lincolnshire player simply could not return well enough often enough to counter the dominant Rusedski serve.

Mark Petchey carried on in the same relaxed but positive style he had shown in establishing his supremacy over Tommy Haas the night before, as he went on to beat the young German regarded in his homeland as their best prospect since Boris Becker 7–6, 6–4, 6–2.

With the exception of Ferreira's defeat, most matches in the men's singles progressed in an orderly pattern. It was far from the same in the ladies' singles where three of those considered most likely to threaten Martina Hingis's dream struggled and six more seeds were eliminated.

The highest-ranked among them was Lindsay Davenport, the tall, sturdy Olympic champion, seeded five, who was beaten 7–5, 6–2 by Denia Chladkova of the Czech Republic. 'She was

better than I expected,' said the clearly stunned American, who had apparently not done sufficient homework.

Brenda Schultz-McCarthy once again failed to do as well as her power and style of play suggests she should at Wimbledon. Having boosted her own fastest serve record of 121.8 mph with a delivery timed at 123 mph against Amy Frazier in the first round, she went into her expensively erratic routine as she lost 6–2, 6–3 to Belgium's Sabine Appelmans.

An impressively solid and aggressive performance by Helena Sukova in beating tenth-seeded former champion Conchita Martinez meant there was bound to be a new winner – but it was not going to be Amanda Coetzer, whom some had been tipping as a dark-horse outsider. She went out in the second round for the fifth time in seven years, being outplayed by the Canadian, Patricia Hy-Boulais.

There were tears in the eyes of Monica Seles as she walked off Centre Court after surviving a tremendous battle with the American, Kristina Brandi, 5–7, 6–3, 6–3, in a match continued from overnight when she had been a set and 3–1 down. It was also further evidence, though, that the former world champion was not the force she would need to be to take the title.

British joy, already widespread, would have been overflowing had Karen Cross, so humbly ranked at 322 on the world computer that she even needed a wild card to compete in the qualifying competition, not let slip a lead of a set and 5–2 against Iva Majoli. It was a fine effort by Cross but, at the end of the fifth game the Croatian, who three weekends earlier had been crowned the new winner of the French Open, received treatment for what seemed an eternity for a back injury which could have forced the fourth seed to default. Instead she battled on, saving a match point at 4–5 in the second set as her game started to flow again. It was by no means a capitulation by Cross. She went for her shots with real will but, as she said, 'It's hard not to feel disappointed having come so close.'

WIMBLEDON

day **7**

MONDAY 30 JUNE

Profiles, pressures and military bearing as everyone did their best to make up for lost time . . . and the added tension always associated with the second week began. Opposite, from the top: Patrick Rafter, Luke Jensen and Monica Seles. Above: A pensive Marcelo Rios. Below: Mary Pierce reflects on the state of her game.

The awkwardness of the shot underlines the crumbling of Monica Seles's game as a joyful Sandrine Testud (right) overcame the 6–0 loss of the first set to achieve a stunning victory over the second seed.

British men to reach the last 16 since Bobby Wilson and Roger Taylor in 1964 would fare again 24 hours later.

Inside, a relative calm descended, especially as most of the matches went in the expected fashion. There was one significant exception, on a day when 35,566, the largest second Monday crowd for four years, poured through the gates: the defeat of second-seeded former runner-up Monica Seles on Court 3 by the 25-year-old, 23rd-ranked French player, Sandrine Testud, 0–6, 6–4, 8–6. The outcome was clearly a surprise, although not equalling the degree of shock when Seles was beaten in the second round by the Slovakian, Katarina Studenikova, a year earlier.

The most unexpected aspect of the contest was not so much that Seles lost, for she had lived dangerously in the previous round and no longer has that air of supremacy in the way she moves or strikes her shots, but the manner in which it turned against her. Having responded to the way Testud had aborted her customary baseline style and been prepared to mix up her game more to take the second set, Seles appeared to have overcome the crisis by the time she started to serve for the match at 5–3 in the final set.

At 0–15 she was aghast to see what she believed was an overhit forehand by Testud over-ruled by umpire Jane Harvey, who declared it a winner. That made it 0–30, instead of 15–15, and Testud's belief suddenly soared again. The decibel level from the Seles throat grew steadily with every two-handed groundstroke and the naturalised American was at her most exasperated when she squandered match point on her opponent's serve before being broken herself at 7–6.

Testud served out in style, starting and finishing the final game with aces and leaving Seles defiantly rejecting suggestions that she will never be able to add the Wimbledon crown to her titles at the three other Grand Slam tournaments. 'I wouldn't be here if I didn't think I could win,' said Seles, although

Outside, when what was still officially Day Seven, even though it was the eighth on which matches had been programmed, began, some of those who had cheered Tim Henman and Greg Rusedski to their victories on Middle Sunday were already queueing to see how the first pair of

Jason Stoltenberg's patient skills gave Yevgeny Kafelnikov (right) more than a few problems before the Russian moved none too convincingly into the fourth round.

the look on her face suggested that other issues, most importantly the serious illness of her father and the extra weight she had been unable to shed, had also taken their toll.

Meanwhile Jana Novotna, still with-

out being at her best, moved into the fourth round comfortably enough against Spanish clay-court specialist Gala Leon Garcia, but the most impressive form of the day in the ladies' singles came from Arantxa Sanchez Vicario as she trounced the Argentinian, Florencia Labat, 6–1, 6–2. By now Sanchez, who would next face Mary Pierce, had dropped only nine games in three matches. For her part, Pierce also showed her best form to date in dismissing another Spaniard, Magui Serna, 6–4, 6–3.

The tempo in the stronger-looking top half of the men's singles draw gathered pace as Pete Sampras and Boris Becker advanced in a manner befitting former champions and Yevgeny Kafelnikov certainly demonstrated the skill, if not yet the consistency, to become one.

One could almost feel Kafelnikov's sense of relief as he eventually completed his 6–3, 7–6, 4–6, 6–3 defeat of Jason Stoltenberg for the Australian was close to the form which carried him unseeded into the semi-finals last year.

With his first serve faltering too often for comfort, it was as well for the third-seeded Russian that the other parts of his game, particularly his volleying, stayed firm, otherwise he could have been heading for much the same fate which befell Seles. Despite the many unforced errors, however, there was more than enough light and shade between the typical big serve and first volley points to provide the crowd with a rich harvest of handsome rallies and make them forget it was the customary time for tea.

Early on it was Kafelnikov's elegant backhand passes which promised to dictate the progress of the match but before long Stoltenberg was also producing backhand returns which were both accurate and well enough disguised to catch his opponent off guard.

In a fascinating second set, Kafelnikov, who served his way out of break points in the fourth and sixth games, looked as if he was a man still with plenty in reserve, almost as if he was testing his range of shots for battles to come.

Pete Sampras, the world champion, was beginning to time his progress to peak form quite nicely, as Zimbabwe's Byron Black was outclassed for the loss of only five games.

Opposite page: Boris Becker (top left) handed out a champion's lesson to Mark Petchey, but despite being back in the top 20 Andrei Medvedev (below left) was spectacularly brought to his knees by Germany's leading teenage prospect, Nicolas Kiefer.

At 4–4, apparently mystified that his lob had missed its target, which it had done by several inches, Kafelnikov seemed to be asking umpire Kim Craven how far it had been out, like a lawn bowler checking the distance of his last delivery from the jack. His next lob, moments later, was played with pin-point precision.

Stoltenberg, 27, contributed an equal share of the inspiring drop shots and other angled-touch winners round the net but it was his returns, not least three on match points, which made this so much a contest for the connoisseur.

Sampras was in ruthlessly efficient form as he dismissed Byron Black, who is a tidy enough player but a lightweight in this company, 6–1, 6–2, 6–2 in 71 minutes. The Zimbabwean could not cope with either the pace or the variety of deliveries from the world champion, who five times ended games with aces and dropped only 12 points on serve.

The American, who, like Becker, had yet to drop a set, clearly enjoyed his first visit this year to the Centre Court, even though he said he had never seen it so chopped up. Similar surprise had been expressed earlier by others, such as Jana Novotna and Tim Henman. 'I'm obviously concerned about the condition of the Centre Court,' said head groundsman Eddie Seaward. 'But we're increasing the air flow through the night with the use of fans, and once the moisture dries out I'm sure the court will become firmer, look better and continue to perform well.' He was right, as usual.

Centre Court receives less light and air movement than other courts because of the shelter provided by the surrounding stands, a problem compounded by the weather, which had meant the covers having to remain on three days and nights in the first week. 'That's the longest I can ever remember the covers having to be on,' said Seaward.

Advocates of a Centre or No. 1 Court roof please note!

While a sterner test for Sampras would be how well he dealt with the serve of Petr Korda, the Czech left-han-

der taken to five sets by one of the few remaining Americans, Alex O'Brien, it was certainly the sort of performance to underline how determined he was to regain the world's most coveted title, which Richard Krajicek had taken from him in the quarter-finals a year earlier.

For his part, Becker, who found No. 1 Court to be harder, with higher bounces, than Centre, also won in a confidently relaxed manner, 6–3, 6–3, 6–2 against British wild card Mark Petchey. 'Boris is in the Premiership and me in the Fourth,' said Petchey, who set about his task in the right aggressive but composed manner, especially to 3–3 in the first set, but a missed forehand volley on the first point of the seventh game, followed by a double fault, provided Becker with the sort of opening he was not likely to reject.

Petchey, who had spent most of the year playing in satellite circuits in far-flung parts of the world and was then looking towards Challenger events in Bristol and Manchester, said, 'The difference between playing at Wimbledon and an Indian satellite is like going to the moon.'

The one seeding upset of the day in the men's matches was provided by Nicolas Kiefer, a protégé of Becker's who reached the last 16 in his first appearance in the main singles with a 6–4, 6–2, 6–4 victory over Andrei Medvedev. Kiefer, 19, who had only officially finished at high school the Monday before The Championships began, had just started as one of the first two players in a Boris Becker squad of young players.

'It's very helpful for me because Boris knows my opponents far better than I do and is able to give me advice for all my matches,' said the teenager, who, unlike his mentor, is happier on the baseline than at the net. The instructions he was given before facing 13th-seeded Medvedev were 'stay cool, look cool and make the last shot in every rally'. He obeyed them to the letter against a talented opponent whose inconsistency again contributed to his downfall and other people's frustration.

WIMBLEDON

day **8**

TUESDAY 1 JULY

The youthful talent of Anna Kournikova (right) overcame the added experience of Helena Sukova but Mary Pierce (below) was crushed in under an hour by the ever-enthusiastic Arantxa Sanchez Vicario.

A day of high drama, enhanced by three rain delays on Centre Court, of 27 minutes, one hour 29 minutes and one hour 14 minutes, earlier in the day, left Tim Henman tantalisingly one set away from joining Greg Rusedski in the quarter-finals when the fast-fading light interrupted his thrilling bid to beat defending champion Richard Krajicek on the Centre Court.

With the crowd roaring their support wildly for the British number one, play was suspended overnight at 8.39 p.m. immediately after Henman, playing his best tennis of the year – and certainly his finest tennis at Wimbledon – had taken a two-sets-to-one lead after two hours and 15 minutes, following three thrilling tie-breaks.

Spare a thought, though, for Sandrine Testud. Hoping to build on her defeat of Monica Seles 24 hours earlier, she was leading fellow French player Nathalie Tauziat 6–4, 6–5, 15–15 when the first deluge arrived. When they resumed, Testud won the next two points to hold match points, before more rain started. 'Just a few more seconds, please!' she cried as the court coverers, eager to protect the grass, nearly trampled on her.

This time the delay was 90 minutes. Tauziat saved the match points, won 11 of the next 12 points to hold two set points of her own but in the end only triumphed 4–6, 7–5, 12–10. Youth overcame experience as Anna Kournikova rallied to beat Helena Sukova 2–6, 6–2, 6–3, while Jana Novotna also recovered from being a set down to beat Mary Joe Fernandez 5–7, 6–4, 7–5 in one of the best matches of the event.

Yet this was a day when, even with Martina Hingis on court, though not kept there very long against Sabine Appelmans, and Aranxta Sanchez Vicario destroying Mary Pierce in under an hour, the ladies were overshadowed by the men – particularly the British men, although the lack of light to complete not only the Henman classic but also former champion Pete Sampras's match with Petr Korda meant that the men's quarter-finals could not take place until at least 48 hours later, instead of getting back on schedule the next day.

Henman came from behind to win the first tie-break 9–7, lost the next, in which he had a set point, by the same margin and then took the third 7–5 after his opponent had saved the first two set points. The 2–1 lead in sets which Henman took home that night at least gave

him the psychological advantage in the eyes of British supporters hoping there would be two home players in the quarter-finals for the first time since Mike Sangster and Bobby Wilson flew the flag so wonderfully in 1961.

Krajicek might well have been 2–1 ahead in sets himself had he not allowed his concentration to be broken when he was fretting about the light early in the middle of the third set. The 6ft 5in fourth seed looked to be taking control through his remarkable serving when he punished Henman for a double fault on break point in the third game by then delivering a whole game of aces, one of them a second serve, another at 135 mph.

After Henman had held to 2–3, Krajicek appealed in vain to Portuguese umpire Jorge Dias that the light was too poor for them to continue. But neither Dias nor referee Alan Mills, watching from just behind the court, looked impressed.

Krajicek was still mumbling and grumbling in the sixth game of the set when, having dropped only five points on his previous eight service games, he started missing first serves. At 30–30, Henman beat him with a glorious forehand pass down the line to set up the vital break-back opportunity which he took with a flashing return to his opponent's feet.

By now the crowd, still filling almost all of the 13,800 seats, was cheering louder than ever, as this set, like the others, was concluded by a tie-break. One mini-break was sufficient. It came on the sixth point when Krajicek was beaten by another fine Henman backhand which dropped in. The Dutchman's look of horror said it all.

The crowd, many of them draped in Union flags or with their faces painted in red, white and blue, must have been beginning to wonder if they would ever see Henman on court after being kept waiting so long by the rain and two earlier

Tim Henman (left) moved within sight of the quarter-finals with an impressive display against defending champion Richard Krajicek on the Centre Court.

During a break between matches, Stefan Edberg's enormous contribution to lawn tennis in general and Wimbledon in particular was recognised when HRH the Duke of Kent, President of the All England Club, presented him with a Waterford Crystal vase in the Royal Box. The Centre Court crowd joined in the congratulations to the London-based Swede, who had won 49 of his 61 singles matches at Wimbledon, the men's singles title twice and the men's doubles title once, in addition to being a wonderful ambassador for his profession.

matches. When they did, they gave him a huge standing, flag-waving reception as the players walked out at 6.18 p.m. And it was not long before their 22-year-old hero gave them added reason to cheer.

Henman's tennis in the first set was the sharpest, most convincing he had produced since the Australian Open. There was no question of his being intimidated by the occasion or his opponent, as he showed when he saved the first break point of the match by racing in with such pace to play a winning drop shot that he was fortunate his shot had bounced twice on Krajicek's side of the court before his momentum left him draped over the net.

Krajicek hit ten aces in the first set but also had to save four set points before losing the tie-break when Henman earned his fifth set point with a whiplash return and took it with a winning forehand. In the second set, Henman's double fault at 4–5 gave Krajicek the opening but in a dramatic climax Henman saved two set points and had one of his own before the Dutchman's 15th ace levelled the match.

Rusedski had reached his first Grand Slam tournament quarter-final by winning the first match of the day on No. 1 Court against Richey Reneberg 7–6, 6–4, 7–6 amid rather less emotion, partly because ticket holders, normally expecting a 2 p.m. rather than noon start to the day, were late arriving but also because his early grip on the match never seriously looked like being broken.

'I think that was one of the best matches I've ever served,' said Rusedski. 'I'm very pleased to be in the quarter-finals but I don't want to stop here,' he added. His 32 aces took his total in the tournament so far to 109, although, as he remarked, well aware of how Goran Ivanisevic hit a record 46 aces in the second round – and lost, 'If I hit aces, that's great, but winning matches is the most important thing.'

Other than in the opening set, when there was a pleasing battle between the power of the Rusedski serve and the often equally intimidating quality of the Reneberg returns, most of the games were starved of rallies. In the 17 games which followed Rusedski's break for 3–2 in the second set until the beginning of the tie-break in the third, there was no glimpse of a break point to stir the emotions and only two games even went to deuce.

Richard Krajicek's serve (left) was a potent force as usual, but with the light fading referee Alan Mills had to decide when to halt play until the following day.

There had just been time for Rusedski to win the opening game, during which he produced a superb lob under pressure to regain the initiative in an exciting rally, and for Reneberg to win his first service point before a passing two-minute shower brought a disconcerting delay of 27 minutes for the players.

When they resumed Rusedski had the first break point of the match in the sixth game but, despite a stretching, long-striding dash from beyond one side of the court to almost the sideline of the other, he was just unable to make another return.

Even so it was a good example of both how well focused and resolute Rusedski felt, qualities reflected again when he rallied from 0–30 in the 11th game of the set after two over-rules which went against him to hold with another serve and then his tenth ace.

The first-set tie-break quickly swung decisively in Rusedski's favour once Reneberg, who was fighting off a chill, missed a backhand lob to go 1–2 down and Rusedski punished him for the lapse by winding himself up to deliver two enormous serves, the first an ace, the other unreturnable, which flew off the frame of his opponent's racket, to maintain his command.

Rusedski rounded off the tie-break 7–2 in a 41-minute set and the aces continued to flow in the next set when there were three in the second game and two in the fourth, before he broke in the fifth, where, after a Reneberg double fault had given him the opportunity, his returns, one aspect of his game where he feels there is room for added consistency, did the rest.

There were times during the third set when Rusedski produced brilliant pick-up half-volleys off his toes that not even John McEnroe, one of the most distinguished left-handers of all time, would have bettered, although they were rare jewels amid an over-abundance now of serve-and-volley points.

Only 12 points were conceded on serve in the 12 games which led to the tie-break, where there was a mini-break apiece before Rusedski, sensing his chance at 4–4, unleashed a flurry of powerful groundstrokes which forced Reneberg eventually to send a return wide. After another winning serve brought up match point, the crowd was willing Rusedski to end it with an ace. He was eager to oblige. The first serve missed by a whisker; the bold second serve did the trick.

Greg Rusedski's sliced backhand returns were as significant as his match-winning serve as he hit peak form in beating Richey Reneberg (below) to reach his first Grand Slam tournament quarter-final.

Nicolas Kiefer followed up his defeat of Andrei Medvedev with an even bigger scalp, third-seeded Yevgeny Kafelnikov (inset), whose woes were not helped when he needed treatment for a leg strain.

The upset of the day in the men's singles was the defeat of third-seeded Yevgeny Kafelnikov, the best outside bet for the title in the eyes of many, by 19-year-old German Nicolas Kiefer. And that meant that Boris Becker was able to walk off Centre Court with a standing ovation ringing in his ears after his 6–2, 6–2, 7–6 defeat of Marcelo Rios straight into a triple celebration.

For almost before the three-times former champion had time to get back into the dressing room and reflect on his success, the equally enormous cheers from Court 2 were telling him that his protégé had also been triumphant. And that, added to the earlier success of another former champion, Michael Stich, playing quite beautifully and entirely free from pressure since announcing his decision to retire in September, meant that for the first time there were three Germans in the last eight.

Kiefer has been dubbed the next Andre Agassi. He regards it as a compliment, even though in addition to his taking the ball as early and hitting it with the same ferocity as the American, an already receding hairline has contributed to the comparison. Willing to go to the net more often than he had been inclined to do in beating Andrei Medvedev the day before, he made it evident from the start that he was ready to take every opportunity he could create in a match in which he had nothing to lose.

It was his relentless pressure on Kafelnikov, lobbing or passing him when he came in or simply beating him with the accuracy and control of his fiercely struck groundstrokes, which upset a player who even Russian journalists said looked as if he had 'got out of the wrong side of the bed'.

Rios was not overawed. Indeed, in the third set, the Chilean demonstrated that he was learning fast how to play on grass but his returns, though often brilliant, could not quite overshadow the dominance of the Becker serve.

Stich struck 25 aces in a typical serve-and-volley shoot-out with Mark Wood-

forde, while in an all-Australian clash Todd Woodbridge's returns helped him defeat Patrick Rafter, the 12th seed. All the time, though, Frenchman Cedric Pioline was still there, a break down in the second and fourth sets to Brett Steven but winning 3–6, 6–3, 6–4, 7–5. It was only because he now had to play Rusedski that anyone other than the French started to take notice.

Not the Sheikh of Araby but former champion Pete Sampras, well protected against the evening chill which prevented his fourth-round match with Petr Korda being finished. Overleaf: Another ovation for Boris Becker, one of Wimbledon's most popular players for more than a decade, after he had moved into the quarter-finals by beating Marcelo Rios.

Not only Tim Henman but also Pete Sampras, leading Petr Korda 6–4, 4–2 overnight, had work to do on the second Wednesday when, in normal weather circumstances, the men would have been playing their quarter-finals and the ladies enjoying a day's rest, at least from singles.

Instead the menu for the day spotlighted those two unfinished fourth-round matches in the men's singles and the quarter-finals of the ladies' singles, which would at least then put them back on track.

Happily for British fans, Henman was the coolest person on the Centre Court during the 36 minutes he needed to complete his defeat of Richard Krajicek, and could then start planning how to tackle Michael Stich, the 1991 champion, in the quarter-finals.

He showed nerveless composure in such testing circumstances in this intimidating arena, once Krajicek had cracked under the pressure by missing four consecutive volleys in succession to go 3–2 down. 'I knew then that the match was there for the taking and I wasn't going to lose it,' said Henman, who, by saving a break-back point at 3–5 with the sort of stunning serve which had been eluding him earlier but was there when it was most needed, went on to his 7–6, 6–7, 7–6, 6–4 triumph.

So, with Greg Rusedski already through to meet Cedric Pioline, Britain had two players in the quarter-finals for the first time since 1961 and there was inevitable speculation about greater deeds which might just follow. For had both of them won – and despite what was to happen, it was not beyond the bounds of possibility – they would then have had to play each other, guaranteeing a British finalist for the first time since Bunny Austin in 1938. For home fans, it was fun to dream while they could.

It was not solely patriotic fervour at work. John McEnroe had already forecast that Henman, with his quick hands and skilfully instinctive mind, had the ability to win Wimbledon and Krajicek, when asked about Henman's chances of

beating Stich, replied, 'If he gets his serve going then he has a good chance.'

Krajicek's reservations stemmed from the Henman double faults which were almost disastrous against his fellow countryman, Paul Haarhuis. The 22-year-old from Oxfordshire, whose strength of character did so much to bring him through that match, acknowledged that he did not serve so well against Krajicek as the night before when he rallied from 1–3 in the third to take home a two-sets-to-one lead.

Krajicek hit the most aces, 24–7, delivered fewer double faults (3–5) and had a higher percentage of winning service returns, but in this match the volleying was the key and that is where Henman, so often opening up the court to earn the chance, won hands down.

'There were a couple of times on big points when he came up with unbelievable volleys and half-volleys,' said Krajicek. 'He doesn't have the power to blow somebody out of the court but if he continues playing the way he has been playing then, although it'll be difficult, he can beat Stich.'

Having saved that one chance Krajicek was offered to redeem what he called 'horrible volleys' in the fifth game of the fourth set, Henman won the six remaining service points he needed to play in glorious style. There was a gasp of alarm when he missed his first serve on his first match point, both from the 13,800 inside the court and thousands more packed on the picnic banks beneath the giant screen outside No. 1 Court. Off the second, though, Krajicek's lofted return invited the forehand volley winner down the line it received – and, except for the Dutchman and his friends, joy was unconfined.

Indeed the biggest cheer inside No. 1 Court, where Sampras was making surprisingly hard work of his 6–4, 6–3, 6–7, 6–7, 6–4 defeat of Korda, before the exciting third-set tie-break, was when Henman's victory was confirmed on the scoreboard.

Sampras had taken only eight minutes

'I only know I'm not going to name my kid Tim – I hate that name.'

Richard Krajicek after his defeat by Tim Henman had ended his tenure as Wimbledon champion.

The seemingly nerveless Tim Henman polished off defending champion Richard Krajicek in style.

Petr Korda (below) needed something more effective than a racket if he was to respond successfully to the final-set form produced by 'Pistol Pete' Sampras.

to complete the second set but Korda hung in well enough to take the third in a tie-break and repeat that success in the fourth, by which time the American was beginning to look lethargic. He was beaten by a forehand pass on the opening point and in next to no time was not only trailing 1–5 but momentarily forgot that it was then time to change ends.

Having lost this tie-break 7–1, Sampras sat in his chair trying to analyse what had gone wrong. He obviously found the answer, although Korda was furious with himself over the double fault and then the missed backhand which cost him his serve in the opening game of the final set. That was enough. Sampras kept that break, completing his victory with his 28th ace.

The best performance in the quarter-finals of the ladies' singles was produced by Anna Kournikova, as she upset Iva Majoli 7–6, 6–4 in a contest which was a difficult one for Nick Bollettieri, watching from the players' box. He has coached them both. Majoli, who spends more time in Florida than her native Croatia, spoke of him as 'my second father' after she won the French Open final. Kournikova says, 'He has helped me so much.'

Perhaps that situation contributed to the nervousness shown by both teenagers, although on the biggest points it was Kournikova, the younger by three years, who demonstrated the greater mental strength. Majoli led 5–3 in the first set but Kournikova's willingness to chase every ball and hit groundstrokes from all parts of the court helped her take three games in succession and then romp through the tie-break 7–1.

The tie-break turned drastically on the fourth point when Majoli made a real hash of what should have been an easy winning volley by striking it wide with the court open. Kournikova, making her singles debut, spoke later of a sore hip which was causing her enough anxiety for her to withdraw from the mixed doubles, where she had been partnering Mark Knowles of the Bahamas. Majoli had another opportunity when she broke in the first game of the second set but a flurry of stunning returns from Kournikova brought an immediate break back.

A larger than usual contingent of Russian journalists could hardly contain their excitement when Kournikova delivered another forceful forehand return

It is not too difficult to spot the quarter-final winners and losers here. Jana Novotna (below left) was overjoyed after beating Yayuk Basuki (below far left), but no more so than Anna Kournikova (below), who danced delightedly to the net to shake hands with her latest victim, Iva Majoli (left). By contrast, victory at this stage was hardly new to Arantxa Sanchez Vicario (right), as she took success against Nathalie Tauziat (far left) in her stride.

down the line to reach match points in the 11th game. Majoli saved the first but was then beaten by a forehand cross-court return. So it was to be Kournikova v. Martina Hingis, the first Wimbledon semi-final between two 16-year-olds. Although Hingis never faced a major threat from Denisa Chladkova – a childhood friend when they both lived in Czecho-slovakia – the 6–3, 6–2 scoreline did not give full merit to the way Chladkova fought in a match of many long rallies.

Jana Novotna moved through to qualify for a semi-final against Arantxa Sanchez Vicario in the other half of the draw, with a 6–3, 6–3 defeat of the Indonesian, Yayuk Basuki, who, despite winning her first four matches in straight sets, could not cope with her more experienced opponent's infinitely stronger serve.

Sanchez went into her match having conceded only 13 games – the least of anyone in the quarter-finals – but Nathalie Tauziat, with nothing to lose and buoyed by her fighting recovery against Sandrine Testud, did everything she could to hustle and harry her by charging to the net, which made for much entertaining play. It was never truly close as Sanchez won 6–2, 7–5, but it was invigorating none the less.

By now, several days later than planned, the doubles were also in full swing and both Sanchez, partnering Hingis, and Novotna, playing with Lindsay Davenport, were soon back on court again. Novotna was already concerned by a sore arm so she was pleased that Fusai and Grande did not detain her un-duly – she and Davenport won 6–1, 6–1. Sanchez and Hingis, on the other hand, then became embroiled in a marathon affair with Chanda Rubin and Brenda Schultz-McCarthy. They won it 13–11 in the third after taking the first tie-break 14–12 and losing the next 8–6. Sanchez was still not finished for the day, although an injury to her brother, Emilio, meant she had to default in the first round of mixed doubles against Britain's Mark Petchey and Clare Wood.

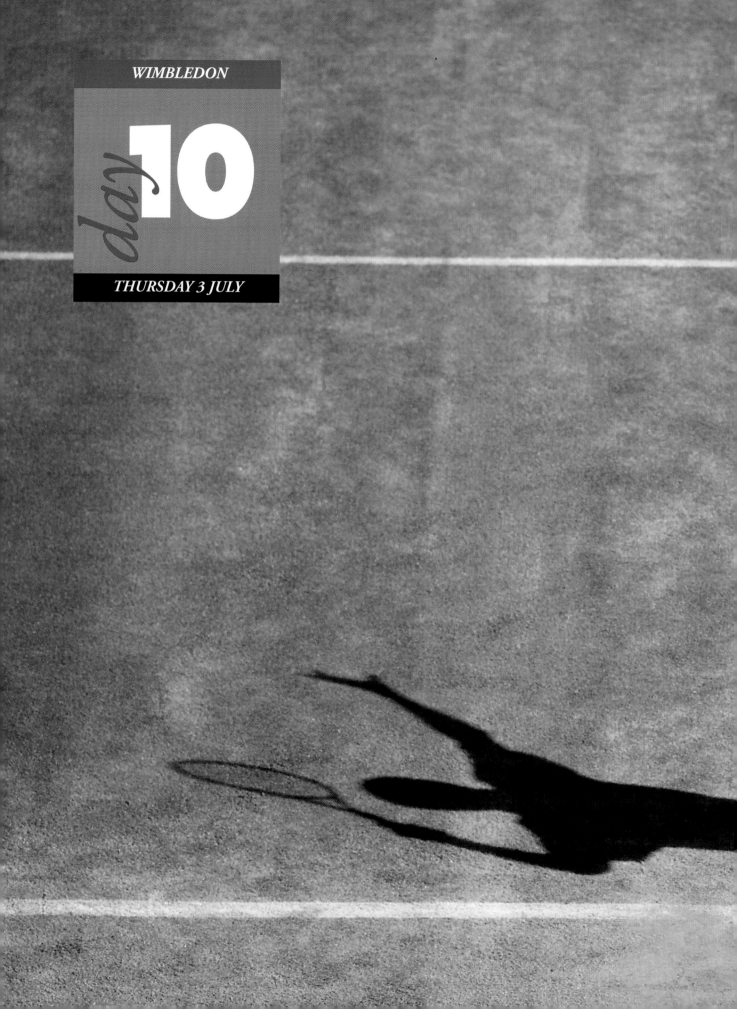

'The dream is over' ran the headlines in British newspapers and broadcast bulletins. And for Tim Henman at least, it had turned into something of a nightmare as both he and Greg Rusedski were outwitted as much as outclassed by two fine grass-court players in their quarter-finals.

Twenty-four hours after he played what he called 'some of the best tennis of my career' to beat defending champion Richard Krajicek, Henman delivered what he admitted was 'some of the worst tennis of my career' as he was crushed 6–3, 6–2, 6–4 in only one hour 28 minutes by former champion Michael Stich. Earlier a tired-looking Rusedski, paying the price, he believed, of 21 matches in the previous 25 days, lost 6–4, 4–6, 6–4, 6–3 to the talented Frenchman, Cedric Pioline, relying just as much on touch as power.

In the broader sense, though, the story of the day came when Boris Becker, as he was shaking hands at the net with Pete Sampras, who had just beaten him 6–1, 6–7, 6–1, 6–4, told his fellow three-times former champion, whom he called 'the best ever' in the game, 'That's it for me here.'

So Becker's 79th singles match at Wimbledon was also his last. The crowd would have remembered it anyway for its many classic serve-and-volley points but even more so now as a landmark in the tournament's history for, as a stunned Sampras said, 'Boris was a part of Wimbledon. This is where he made his mark. The Centre Court was like his living room out there. I feel kind of honoured in a way that I was his opponent in his last match here.'

'The tournament made me. It's always been my favourite and I've always loved to come back here and do well but now I feel like a free man,' said one of the game's most flamboyant and often acrobatic entertainers. The typically swashbuckling manner in which Becker recovered from 3–5 to take the second-set tie-break with four consecutive points was testimony to his ability and continuing spirit but it was the way Sampras swiftly doused the German's renewed fire which reinforced the view he had come to earlier that he no longer had what it takes to win a Grand Slam.

'I feel it's the right moment for me. I don't want to come back being number 60 in the world and praying that I win a couple of rounds. That's not my style. I'm the type of guy who goes into a tournament

Boris Becker says farewell to his beloved Centre Court. After losing to Pete Sampras, seen serving on the previous pages, the German confided to his opponent, when congratulating him on his victory, that it had been his last match at The Championships. Opposite: Becker in typical service action.

Tim Henman's fine run came to an end when Michael Stich (right) produced an immaculate all-court performance to reach the semi-finals.

with a chance to win it. That's not possible any more in Grand Slams. I feel I've come to the end with my head help up high, still playing good tennis. I always wanted to go out on top and that's where I feel right now.'

It was the end of the road also, though only for this year, for Becker's protégé, Nicolas Kiefer, as he was beaten 7–6, 2–6, 6–0, 6–4 by Todd Woodbridge, 26, who dominated around the net, where his agility and lightness of touch, as well as his control, won him many points he might otherwise have lost.

Both British players had exceeded expectations in the way they had competed to reach the last eight, so the degree of disappointment round the new No. 1 Court needed to be kept in perspective. What was inescapable, though, was that in both matches the added experience as well as the broader range of skills demonstrated first by Pioline and then by Stich proved crucial.

There was a gruesome similarity in the pattern of play. Neither Henman nor Rusedski could match their opponents in the two basic requirements for success playing on grass – the serve and the return. Worse still, both contributed greatly to their own problems, not least with double faults.

Henman, who at least had an almost full crowd to encourage him – by no means only the holders of debenture and hospitality seats missed Rusedski's defeat – did not look nervous at the start when he held a break point against the opening Stich service game before intermittent brief showers meant a delay of two hours 43 minutes after one point of the second game. Yet it was not long once they resumed before one sensed there was not the same zip, fluency or control in Henman's game, especially on serve, as there had been against Krajicek or in the 14–12 final set of his third-round defeat of Paul Haarhuis.

The worst fears began to rise when, at 3–4 in the first set, Henman double-faulted twice in trailing 0–40 and, despite rallying to 30–40, then double-faulted again to leave the increasingly impressive and immaculate German to serve out for the first set. Another double fault was the opening for Stich to gain the first of two breaks as he twisted the knife in the second set.

'On grass my whole attacking game is going to be based a lot round my serve and I served particularly poorly today

and that then rubs off on other parts of your game,' said Henman, 'Everything which could go wrong did go wrong and that's without looking at the way Michael played. He played well but there wasn't so much for him to do.'

Apart from his break point in the first game, Henman's only other chance of denting his opponent's serve had come and gone, thanks to another perfect serve-and-volley point by Stich, in the fourth game of the second set. The British number one was clutching at straws. Although Stich missed first serves fairly often, his second serve, especially the kicker high into his opponent's backhand, was still the most effective in the game.

Henman was perhaps a shade un-lucky in the way he was broken in the seventh game of the third set. Just as he went to hit what was one of his best serves for some time, Stich put his hand up because a pigeon dropped down from the roof behind the server. When the point was replayed, Stich's stinging re-turn was volleyed over the baseline by Henman and a perfect service game two games later was too little and too late.

'I played very smart tactically,' said Stich, who was beginning to wonder if the record-breaking delays during the fortnight, much the same as when he won the title in 1991, might be an omen. He praised Henman's all-court ability but felt he made 'a big tactical error and never gave himself a chance to get into the match by staying back on the second serves. That told me "Now he's in trouble. He's somewhere in the no-man's land where he doesn't really know what to do." '

The serve which had underpinned Rusedski's progress to his first Grand Slam tournament quarter-final also clearly deserted him at his hour of greatest need. It was not just the sprinkling of double faults which he perpetrated, especially two in a terrible opening game for the left-hander, which meant he was immediately having to try and catch up. His predica-ment was made worse because he was un-able to make Pioline, a former US Open

Cedric Pioline (left) was one opponent too many for Britain's Greg Rusedski, whose disappointment is evident as he waves his thanks to the spectators who gave him so much support.

Opposite: Todd Woodbridge is ecstatic after beating Nicolas Kiefer.

runner-up, once in the top ten but now an under-rated 88 in the world rankings, play enough with his returns.

Although Rusedski raised hopes by winning the second set, the sustained quality, and often the stunning power, of the Frenchman's returns meant the pressure was increasingly one way, especially as the British left-hander's percentage of first serves remained so low. 'My return of serve was the key,' said Pioline. 'When I hit those really big shots, he was a little discouraged.'

Rusedski said he was disappointed that he had not played better for the crowd and added, 'It was a case of the mind wanting to do my best and the body saying no.

Cedric took advantage and played some great tennis. His returns are probably the best in the world. Not many guys take a 138 [mph] serve down the tee and crack it for a winner on break point.'

Inevitably, in such circumstances, the semi-finals of the ladies' singles were overshadowed, although, in the event, neither was a nail-biting contest. With Martina Hingis concerned that her serve lacked pentration and Anna Kournikova increasingly conscious of a painful right hip, not to mention the rain delays, the tennis was too often erratic. Kournikova hit the greater number of elegant winners but also made far more mistakes as Hingis beat her 6–3, 6–2.

Novotna–Sanchez provided a much higher quality of play and one could sense the 'needle' between two players who had both been caustically critical of each other the day before. The rallies were long and fierce but Novotna, who had stood her ground against suggestions that the match should be switched to No. 1 Court in case Becker and Sampras went to five sets, was both the more resourceful and the more determined. Her powerful volleys and confident overheads finally broke even Sanchez's running and resolve. It meant the final would be the one most had predicted – and wanted.

Martina Hingis (above) celebrates becoming the youngest finalist in the ladies' singles this century with victory over fellow 16-year-old Anna Kournikova, watched by former US President George Bush and his wife Barbara, sitting alongside Anne Curry, whose husband, John, is Chairman of the All England Club.

Opposite: Mark Philippoussis waits at the net, ready to pounce on the return of the serve by his partner, Pat Rafter, but their efforts were in vain against Jacco Eltingh and Paul Haarhuis.

What a difference a day makes. Barely 24 hours after declaring, 'I didn't come here to retire, I came to win The Championships,' Michael Stich lost 6–7, 6–2, 6–2, 5–7, 6–4 to 44th-ranked Frenchman Cedric Pioline and then went even further than Boris Becker the day before by announcing that he had played for the last time not only at Wimbledon but also on the tour.

In a dramatic climax to a wonderfully exciting and fiercely competitive contest lasting two minutes under three hours, Stich had been outclassed by Pioline, who, though no better than a 100–1 shot at the start of the tournament, therefore became the first Frenchman to reach the final since Yvon Petra, the last champion to wear long trousers, when he won the title in 1946.

Pioline therefore became the lowest-ranked player since New Zealander Chris Lewis (82) in 1983 to put himself at least within clutching distance of one of the most famous sporting trophies in the world. He had lost all seven of his previous matches against top-seeded former champion Pete Sampras, including the 1993 final of the US Open, taking only two sets in the process.

That mattered little to him after the greatest win and almost certainly the finest match of his career. 'I'm so happy. I was so nervous when it went to a fifth set because I've lost some long matches before that. I'm also so tired that I just want to go back to the hotel and sleep,' he added in that softly spoken manner which, like his almost lumbering gait, belied admirable speed and strength. 'Although Pete's beaten me seven times, maybe it's my turn this time,' he added hopefully.

Stich, who lost his composure and also, for a while, the support of the crowd with moments of petulance, rallied from two sets to one down to force a decider but then undermined that effort by double-faulting to lose the opening game of the final set. Yet, encouraged by the way his opponent had missed a crucial overhead in the last game of the fourth set, he continued to chase and harry Pioline to the end, sensing that the Frenchman, who had needed treatment to a strained shoulder in the second set, was tiring. 'In the fifth set I was close every time and had the feeling that if I had been able to break back in the tenth game [when Pioline double-faulted to 15–30] I could

Cedric Pioline (left) emerged triumphant from an enthralling five-set battle with Michael Stich (below) to reach his second Grand Slam tournament final.

have won it 7–5,' he claimed, not un-reasonably.

Stich, the 1991 Wimbledon champion, described the atmosphere as 'fantastic. The adrenalin kept us both going. At times it was as if our bodies were on court but our minds were floating. Matches like this are very rare. I was very happy to be part of this one.'

It was not long before the crowd could appreciate how Pioline and Stich, who had his stomach muscles heavily strapped, came to beat the British heroes, Greg Rusedski and Tim Henman, the day before. Serves and returns were again of the highest quality, with the volleying no less convincing – and it stayed that way for almost the whole of what became second only to Henman v. Haarhuis as the most gripping, as well as the most exciting, men's match of the fortnight. It was the perfect answer to those who suggest a grass-court match between two big servers *has* to be boring.

Pioline's fighting spirit and determination on the day were never in doubt, especially in the tenth game of the opening set when he saved four set points. On the third of them, Stich hit a firm enough return which in many instances would have been a crosscourt winner but Pioline threw himself full length to play one of those diving forehand returns on which, presumably, Boris Becker's copyright had just expired.

The three-times former champion, who had announced that this was his final Wimbledon appearance after losing to Pete Sampras the night before, was back at Wimbledon, principally to clear his dressing room locker, but he dallied long enough to offer Stich advice as to the tactics he should try to employ against the Frenchman. If it was along the lines of the 'stay cool, look cool' guidance Becker had given his 'apprentice' Nicolas Kiefer, the message was forgotten in the second and third sets. Although Stich dominated the first-set tie-break, which he rounded off 7–2 with an ace, his irritation over a few line-calls began to detract from the way he

had been playing in the second and third sets, leaving him too tough a recovery hill to climb.

The weather was still pretty gloomy but there were glimpses of sunshine for Americans on the Fourth of July in the way Sampras demonstrated his supremacy with a 6–2, 6–1, 7–6 defeat of Todd Woodbridge. As the score indicates, the Sampras power was too much for an opponent who tried every trick he knew, not least taking the power off his chipped returns and hoping that it might provoke an unforced volley error or at least give him the room to attempt a pass with his next shot.

In the event such hopes were only scantily realised and for the first two sets Woodbridge must have been aching for the backing of his doubles partner, Mark Woodforde, who was restricted to offering moral support from the players' box. As smartly and positively as Woodbridge had played in reaching his first Grand Slam tournament semi-final, especially against fellow Australian Pat Rafter in the fourth round and Michael Chang in the first, this time he was in a different league.

Just briefly, in the third set, when Woodbridge broke back to 2–2, he had something to smile about. That was the first time Sampras had lost his serve in 97 service games, stretching back to the first round against Sweden's Mikael Tillstrom. Woodbridge persisted to force a tie-break but a missed backhand volley on the 17th stroke of the fifth point gave Sampras the chance he needed to end a losing sequence of three tie-breaks, 7–3.

On the doubles front, Paul Haarhuis and Jacco Eltingh, winners over the years of the Australian, French and US Open titles, but hitherto never better than quarter-finalists at Wimbledon, reached the final of the men's event with a comprehensively efficient 6–2, 6–2, 6–4 victory over Martin Damm and Pavel Vizner. In the previous round the pair from the Czech Republic had closed the door on domestic interest with their fighting recovery to beat Neil Broad and South African Piet Norval 4–6, 4–6, 7–6, 6–3, 6–4.

Todd Woodbridge (left) tried all he knew, though in vain, to divert Pete Sampras from his familiar path but was thrilled, none the less, to have demonstrated that he can be a threat at Wimbledon in both singles and doubles.

Above: For Woodbridge (right), just being on the Centre Court in the semi-final against Sampras (opposite) had been an occasion and an experience to cherish.

Broad, though, remained the last British player in any of the five main events when he and another South African partner, Mariaan de Swardt, having already eliminated the sixth seeds, Sandon Stolle and Mary Joe Fernandez, beat the last remaining all-British partnership, Danny Sapsford and Shirli-Ann Siddall, 7–5, 6–3 in the third round of the mixed doubles.

Gigi Fernandez and Natasha Zvereva, hoping to add to the three consecutive titles they had won in the ladies' doubles from 1992 to '94, reached the semi-finals with a 5–7, 6–4, 6–4 victory over Mary Joe Fernandez and Lisa Raymond, but Jana Novotna, one of their final opponents in each of their triumphant years, withdrew. Increasingly worried by the stomach muscle she had pulled slightly the day before and determined not to take undue risk for the ladies' singles final, she and Lindsay Davenport gave Sabine Appelmans and Miriam Oremans a walkover into the penultimate round.

day **12**

The sun was shining brightly at last as Jana Novotna and Martina Hingis posed for the photographers before the start of the ladies' singles final.

This time there were no tears from Jana Novotna when she was beaten again in the final of the ladies' singles, just admiration, shared by everyone who watched the match, for the most remarkably gifted champion for her age the game has ever seen.

After winning her semi-final, Martina Hingis, still more than two months short of her 17th birthday, had declared, 'I hate grass and I hate the court because I have to think so differently.' By the end of this first day of The Championships to be bathed in glorious sunshine, all such thoughts had been banished.

Novotna, who received a noticeably warmer and louder reception than the new champion when she was persuaded to take a lap of honour after her 2–6, 6–3, 6–3 defeat, sighed, 'I did my best, I went down fighting, but she was just the better player today.' Hingis, as she had proved with increasing emphasis from the Australian Open through to Wimbledon, had become the better player against almost everyone on any surface . . . every day, as one by one the game's records, in terms of the youngest achievers, had fallen to her.

Hingis led Novotna 3–2 in previous matches but this was their first on grass, where the Czech was expected to have the advantage. There was no surprise in the way Novotna, 28, set about her task. She was out of her blocks to the net like an Olympic sprinter, not only behind her own first and second serves but when she was returning as well, and with only eleven minutes on the Centre Court clock she was leading 4–0. 'I felt like a beginner,' Hingis admitted. 'I didn't know what to do. I just wanted to hold my serve so that she knew I could play.'

In the fifth game, Hingis did just that and, although Novotna continued to look dominant as she tucked away the opening set in 19 minutes, there were already the initial signs that the Swiss youngster was not going to be swept aside on the high tide of sentimenal support for her seasoned opponent. The aftermath of Novotna's defeat by Steffi Graf in the 1993 final, after she had led

4–1, with a point for 5–1, in the third set, and then cried her eyes out on the comforting shoulder of HRH the Duchess of Kent during the presentation ceremony, is now part of tennis folklore. Hingis is named after one tennis legend, Martina Navratilova. The feeling as Wimbledon '97 drew to a close was that she is destined to become another.

The coolness with which she astutely worked out how to find her way back into the match after Novotna had produced surely one of the best opening sets anyone has played in the ladies' final was almost scary for one so young. Naturally it was a pity, not just for Novotna but for the contest as well, that early in the second set the third seed began to be restricted, especially on serve, by the pulled stomach muscle she had suffered 48 hours earlier.

Had Novotna been able to continue serving powerfully and darting to the net to put away overheads and volleys with the same impressive authority as in the first set, then everything might still have been fine for her. Yet not only did the serve start to lose much of its sting but first volleys were not being put away any more and too many of Novotna's returns of all kinds were starting to give her opponent too many opportunities to reveal the devastating strength, accuracy and control of her double-handed backhands. The situation called for at least a re-think.

'I went into the match knowing that

Jana Novotna (left) started brilliantly but by early in the second set the inspired tennis produced by Martina Hingis (below) was starting to turn things round.

If there was one shot above all others which made Martina Hingis the champion, it was the devastating double-handed backhand which kept passing her opponent.

Martina was either going to win it or lose it because I wouldn't change my style, that I would be aggressive and keep coming in,' said Novotna. Admirable though that might sound normally, a Wimbledon final, as Arthur Ashe demonstrated in his brilliant strategical triumph over Jimmy Connors in the 1975 final, can be one of the smartest times to change the tactical direction, if only to keep the opponent guessing. And Hingis, by the start of the second set, knew exactly what shot to expect, where and when.

Confirmation that the match was starting to turn against Novotna came in the sixth game of the second set. For the first time, Novotna was taken to deuce in a game during which both had been 'gifting' each other winners. But the chance Novotna then offered Hingis to hit another of those sweeping backhand winners for the break was critical.

Perhaps the most significant among the winning Hingis backhands was the running shot she produced down the line to save the point which would have given Novotna a 3–0 lead in the final set. That might have been enough to make her forget the pain. But then came two more brilliant passes as Hingis held for 4–2 as, despite one more flurry of courageous defiance from Novotna, she went on to become the first player from Switzerland to win a Wimbledon singles championship.

A sharply taken forehand crosscourt winner which ended the match also made Hingis the first former junior Wimbledon champion (1994) to triumph in the main event as well since Ann Jones, whose successes were achieved in 1956 and 1969. 'In the beginning I didn't know what to do,' she said. 'I just had to keep cool. Now it's a dream come true. Winning Wimbledon means you're going to be remembered for ever,' she said before adding, wistfully, 'Maybe I'm too young to win this title.'

Post-match celebrations for Hingis were severely curtailed for she had to return to the courts twice later in the day, winning one round of mixed doubles, inevitably the event worst delayed by the first week's weather, and then reappearing for the quarter-final, in which she looked exhausted as she and South African John-Laffnie De Jager were beaten 5–7, 6–3, 6–4 by Neil Broad and Marianne de Swardt.

Her ladies' doubles interest this year had ended 48 hours earlier when she and Aranxta Sanchez Vicario were beaten 6–4, 5–7, 6–2 by the American-Dutch combination of Nicole Arendt and Manon Bollegraf, who then went on to reach the final with another three-sets victory, this time 6–2, 3–6, 6–1 over Larisa Neiland of Latvia and Helena Sukova from the Czech Republic,

Hingis's triumphant partner in the event a year earlier.

Ready to dispute the trophy with them were former champions Gigi Fernandez and Natasha Zvereva, while in the men's doubles Todd Woodbridge and Mark Woodforde took their now customary place in the final with a 7–6, 6–4, 3–6, 6–3 defeat of two other redoubtable doubles performers, Wayne Black and Jim Grabb. It was a match spread over two days, causing the men's doubles final to be postponed until the final Sunday.

One other final was decided. Jo Durie, in between her spells in the BBC Television commentary box, and Anne Smith came through Group A of the 35 and over ladies' invitation doubles and then beat the more seasoned stalwarts, Wendy Turnbull and Virginia Wade, both also now regular tennis commentators on television, 6–2, 6–1.

Left: The joy and despair as Hingis became the youngest ladies' singles champion in modern times, leaving Jana Novotna runner-up for a second time.

Anne Smith and Jo Durie, on the baseline, on their way to winning the 35 and over ladies' invitation doubles.

No tears from Jana Novotna. 'She was the better player on the day,' she acknowledged as she stood alongside Sir Geoffrey Cass, President of the Lawn Tennis Association, as John Curry chatted to the beaming champion while umpire Jeremy Shales was presented to the Duke and Duchess of Kent. Then it was time for Hingis (right) to begin her lap of honour.

As a schoolboy, Pete Sampras used to say his lifetime ambition was to play well enough to be regarded as a right-handed Rod Laver. Most watching him outplay Frenchman Cedric Pioline so comprehensively on the Centre Court in the 1997 final were convinced that the dream had been realised. For sustained quality, by no means restricted solely to his serve, the tennis he produced for his 6–4, 6–2, 6–4 victory was arguably his best of the four finals which have already made Sampras, still only 25, a four-times champion at Wimbledon, against four different opponents.

Having started the fortnight as 7–4 favourite in the betting, Sampras went into the final at 1–4 and, in keeping with their well-known generous nature, the bookmakers then had already decided not to offer better than evens against him joining Bjorn Borg one year hence as the only five-times winners since The Challenge Round was abolished in 1922.

For once it was difficult to argue with them. Although Borg was 24 when he won his fifth title, the signs of weariness were then beginning to show. The impression from Sampras as he started to enjoy the regaining of the trophy he won three years in succession between 1993 and '95 at The Champions' Dinner that evening, joining chairman John Curry with a Churchillian-size cigar, was that he has already set his eye on even more. With another £415,000 to add to around £18m he has already won in prize money – a figure almost certainly trebled by endorsements – he hardly needed further financial temptations as an incentive.

The next most immediate record then within grasp would be to become winner of the most singles titles at the four Grand Slam tournaments. He already held more than any other active player on the tour and his one hour 34 minutes triumph on this occasion, equalling the time it took Richard Krajicek to beat MaliVai Washington a year earlier, placed him level on the all-time list with fellow American Bill Tilden with ten.

Only Laver, who was at Wimbledon for the opening of the new No. 1 Court on the first day of The Championships but returned to California during the second week, and Borg, on 11 Grand Slam titles, plus Roy Emerson, with 12, were then still ahead of him.

However much Sampras may be criticised for lacking charisma on court, it takes someone with exceptional skill, confidence, ability and determination to hold his serve all but twice in the 118 games in which he had served in seven matches involving 24 sets over the fortnight, especially as the rain meant cramming five of those matches into the second week.

Even before the final, which was more of a masterclass than a match, began, 44th-ranked Pioline, unseeded and, at 100–1 two weeks earlier, certainly under-rated, must have felt as if Mount Everest would have to be conquered for him to become the first French winner since Yvon Petra in 1946. When he double-faulted on the first point and was broken in the third game, in which Sampras produced three of those stunning returns with which he had beaten Todd Woodbridge and Boris Becker in the two previous rounds, he must have felt he was being asked to do it without oxygen.

Pioline kept trying, though with the increasing thought that it was a hopeless task. There was a little bounce of exhilaration along the baseline after a brilliant backhand top-spin lob which momentarily checked the world champion as he was serving for the first set. The response, almost like a reprimand, was the one Sampras so often supplies in such circumstances – an ace, his fifth in what went on to become a match total of 17 and 119 for the fortnight.

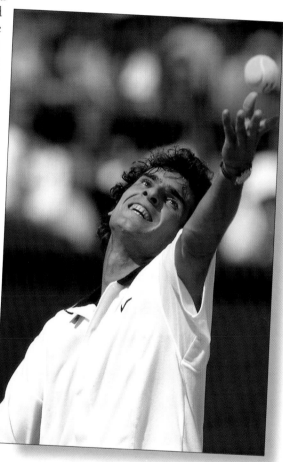

Cedric Pioline was soon under intense pressure and desperately needing to hold all his service games when he began the men's singles final against Pete Sampras.

Sampras, who beat Carlos Moya in the Australian Open final in January and Michael Chang in the US Open final last September, also in straight sets, was even more 'in the zone', as he calls it, in the second set. Having broken for 3–2, he hit three consecutive aces at the start of the next game and the bewildered Pioline then must have wanted to crawl away and hide when he missed three terrible volleys – the sort he had been putting away so effectively in earlier rounds – to trail 2–5.

Pioline collected only four points off the Sampras serve in the opening set; just three in the second. And having returned better, without reward, in the second game of the third set than at any other time in the match, to then lose his own serve to love meant he could only grin and bear it. Sampras, who described his quarter-final defeat of Boris Becker as the biggest match for him – 'the only one I feared' – wobbled for a moment or two in the eighth game of this set when he actually double-faulted to give Pioline his only break point in the match but the Frenchman could do nothing with his next return.

The crowd, having paid £54 for a seat, naturally wanted a longer, more competitive match but at least they were treated to another virtuoso performance from a champion who, once he had recovered from a frightening situation when, from two sets up, he was pushed to a final set by Petr Korda in the fourth round, yet again brought his game to a peak at precisely the right time and in the right place.

Just as Sampras's talent has earned him a season ticket to make a winner's tour of the Centre Court with the trophy – he had to be restrained by chief executive Christopher Gorringe from dashing round too quickly this time – so the Woodies, aka Todd Woodbridge and Mark Woodforde, have become regular visitors to the Royal Box, where the doubles and other trophies are usually presented. They were there for a fifth consecutive time, thereby equalling the 96-year-old record held by the British

duo, Laurie and Reggis Doherty, between 1897 and 1901.

In the final, the Australians made it business as usual when they came through an emotionally testing battle with Paul Haarhuis and Jacco Eltingh, immediately behind them in the doubles rankings, 7–6, 7–6, 5–7, 6–3. Having

The variety, as much as the power and accuracy, of the Sampras serve continued to keep Cedric Pioline (below) on the run.

Pete Sampras acknowledges the appreciation of the crowd before kissing the trophy, which was then engraved with his name for a fourth time while he was being interviewed for NBC television in the United States by John McEnroe. Below left: Commiserations for Cedric Pioline from the Duke and Duchess of Kent.

Gigi Fernandez turns, ready to embrace her partner, Natasha Zvereva, after they won the ladies' doubles for the fourth time in six years.

Opposite: Wesley Whitehouse of South Africa and Carla Black of Zimbabwe on their way to winning the junior singles titles.

fought back from 2–4 to win the first set after 41 minutes in a 7–4 tie-break and scraped through a second tie-break 9–7, Woodbridge, 26, and Woodforde, 31, the best player on court, should have won in straight sets. They led 5–3, 40–0 in the third but Woodbridge had a nightmare service game and they lost not just four match points in that game but four games in succession.

The fourth set also saw the Aus-tralians lead 5–2, with Woodbridge to serve at 5–3, but this time the right-handed member of a superb partnership played a brilliant forehand volley to reach 40–15 and all signs of nerves vanished. Overjoyed at the end, they celebrated by hitting balls into the crowd and then aimed them towards their emotionally proud coach, Ray Ruffels, until he caught and kept one as a souvenir.

Celebrations too from Gigi Fernandez and Natasha Zvereva, who won the ladies' doubles for the fourth time in six years after re-forming their partnership in the spring. 'This victory means as much as the first we won in 1993,' said Fernandez following their 7–6, 6–4 defeat of Nicole Arendt and Manon Bollegraf. Zvereva added, 'To come back and immediately win two Grand Slam titles, the French and then this, is pretty special. I think we've amazed ourselves.' The top seeds, who dropped only one set in six matches, had to come from 2–4 behind in the first-set tie-break to win it 7–4 when Bollegraf gave it away with two double faults. The match remained even in the second set until Bollegraf was broken in the seventh game.

The only top seeds not to win their event in 1997 were the mixed doubles pair of Grant Connell and Lindsay Davenport. In what was to be Connell's last match at Wimbledon, they were beaten 3–6, 6–2, 6–3 by the brother and sister partnership of Cyril Suk and Helena Sukova, who went on to retain the title 4–6, 6–3, 6–4 against Andrei Olhovskiy and Larisa Neiland. They in turn had ended the hopes of Britain's former South African, Neil Broad, and Marianne De Swardt 7–6, 4–6, 6–3 in the other semi-final.

It was 8.45 p.m. before Suk and Sukova were presented with their trophy on the new No. 1 Court by the President of the All England Club, HRH the Duke of Kent, but they showered, changed and dashed to the Savoy quickly enough to enjoy a deserved ovation as they wended their way through the room to their table.

Carla Black from Zimbabwe, sister of

Byron and Wayne, scored a double success in the junior girls' singles and doubles. In the singles, where she was seeded three, she completed a succession of straight-sets victories with a 6–3, 7–5 defeat of the American, Aubrie Rippner, while in the doubles final she and Irina Selyutina from Kazakhstan recovered from losing the first set to beat Majo Matevic and Katarina Srebotnik from Slovenia 3–6, 7–5, 6–3.

The most successful British player in the girls' singles was unseeded Hannah Collin, who beat Srebotnik, the second seed, on her way to the quarter-finals, where she was beaten 6–1, 6–4 by the sixth-seeded runner-up, Rippner. Among British boys, Adrian Barnes did best, reaching the third round, where he was beaten 6–2, 6–1 by the powerfully built, top-seeded German, Daniel Elsner, who, like Carla Black, had won the junior singles at the French Open. His double hopes were ended when he lost 6–3, 7–6 in the final to South African Wesley Whitehouse, who was also runner-up with Jaco Vande Westhuizen in the boys' doubles, the pair losing 6–4, 6–2 to South Americans Luis Horna of Peru and Nicolas Massu of Chile.

Age, according to several of their teasing rivals, was a major factor as Jeremy Bates and India's Ramesh Krishnan won a well-contested 35 and over gentlemen's invitation doubles championship 6–4, 6–4 in the final against two former South Africans (now both Americans), Kevin Curren and Johan Kriek, while Jaime Fillol from Chile and Dick Stockton of the United States, both barely looking old enough to be in the 45 and over category, won the final of that event 6–1, 6–2 from Australian Owen Davidson and South African Cliff Drysdale.

So Wimbledon '97 came to a close. And as Club chairman John Curry said, after paying tribute to everyone who had contributed to the way The Championships had overcome so many problems from the weather, 'That's All, Folks. That really is the end of Wimbledon '97 . . . Phew!'

A fifth successive men's doubles title for Todd Woodbridge and Mark Woodforde.

The sun-baked Centre Court crowd had been treated to a classic demonstration of near-perfect tennis from the most complete men's singles champion for many years.

The Ladies' Doubles Championship
Gigi Fernandez & Natasha Zvereva

The Ladies' Singles Championship
Martina Hingis

The Mixed Doubles Championship
Cyril Suk & Helena Sukova

The 35 and over Gentlemen's Invitation Doubles
Jeremy Bates & Ramesh Krishnan

The 35 and over Ladies' Invitation Doubles
Anne Smith & Jo Durie

The 45 and over Gentlemen's Invitation Doubles
Jaime Fillol & Dick Stockton

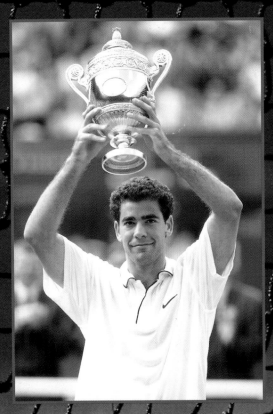

The Gentlemen's Singles Championship
Pete Sampras

The Gentlemen's Doubles Championship
Todd Woodbridge & Mark Woodforde

The Boys' Singles Championship
Wesley Whitehouse

The Boys' Doubles Championship
Luis Horna & Nicolas Massu

The Girls' Doubles Championship
Irina Selyutina & Carla Black

The Girls' Singles Championship
Carla Black

CHAMPIONSHIP RECORDS

1997

ALPHABETICAL LIST OF COMPETITORS

LADIES

Adams Miss K.M. (USA)
22 Ahl Miss L.A. (Great Britain)
11 Appelmans Miss S. (Belgium)
7 Arendt Miss N.J. (USA)
4 Barabanschikova Miss O. (Belarus)
Barclay Miss C.G. (Australia)
74 Basuki Miss Y. (Indonesia)
3 Begerow Miss P. (Germany)
Bobkova Miss R. (Czech Republic)
Bollegraf Miss M.M. (Netherlands)
79 Boogert Miss K. (Netherlands)
126 Brandi Miss K. (USA)
Brioukhovets Miss E. (Russia)
13 Cacic Miss S. (USA)
103 Callens Miss E.S.H. (Belgium)
72 Carlsson Miss A. (Sweden)
29 Chladkova Miss D. (Czech Republic)
65 Coetzer Miss A.J. (South Africa)
44 Courtois Miss L. (Belgium)
100 Cristea Miss C. (Romania)
37 Cross Miss K.M. (Great Britain)
Csurgo Miss V. (Hungary)
32 Davenport Miss L.A. (USA)
De Lone Miss E.R. (USA)
de Swardt Miss M. (South Africa)
62 De Ville Miss S. (Belgium)
10 Dechaume-Balleret Mrs A. (France)
43 Dechy Miss N. (France)
34 Diaz Oliva Miss M. (Argentina)
110 Dopfer Miss S. (Austria)
17 Dragomir Miss R. (Romania)
19 Ellwood Miss A. (Australia)
89 Endo Miss M. (Japan)
15 Farina Miss S. (Italy)
28 Feber Miss N. (Belgium)
41 Fernandez Miss G. (USA)
81 Fernandez Miss M.J. (USA)
14 Frazier Miss A. (USA)
Freye Miss K. (Germany)
66 Fusai Miss A. (France)
99 Gagliardi Miss E. (Switzerland)
Garrone Miss L. (Italy)
36 Gersi Miss A. (Czech Republic)
18 Glass Miss A. (Germany)
9 Golarsa Miss L. (Italy)
76 Gorrochategui Miss I. (Argentina)
Graham Miss D.A. (USA)
102 Grande Miss R. (Italy)
125 Grossman Miss A. (USA)
70 Grzybowska Miss M. (Poland)
114 Guse Miss K-A. (Australia)
50 Habsudova Miss K. (Slovakia)
21 Helgeson Nielsen Mrs G. (USA)
1 Hingis Miss M. (Switzerland)
52 Hiraki Miss R. (Japan)
Horn Miss L. (South Africa)
64 Huber Miss A. (Germany)
68 Hy-Boulais Mrs P. (Canada)
63 Inoue Miss H. (Japan)
Jeyaseelan Miss S. (Canada)
Jones Miss D.J. (Australia)
31 Jones Mrs T.S. (USA)
120 Kandarr Miss J. (Germany)
78 Kijimuta Miss N. (Japan)
30 Kleinova Miss S. (Czech Republic)
58 Kournikova Miss A. (Russia)
2 Kremer Miss A.L. (Luxemburg)
Krizan Miss T. (Slovenia)
61 Kruger Miss J. (South Africa)
Kunce Mrs K. (Australia)
101 Labat Miss F. (Argentina)
Lake Miss V. (Great Britain)
8 Langrova Miss P. (Czech Republic)
Lee Miss J. (USA)
90 Leon Garcia Miss G. (Spain)
94 Likhovtseva Miss E. (Russia)
105 Lubiani Miss F. (Italy)
Lugina Miss O. (Ukraine)
Lutrova Miss J. (Russia)
33 Majoli Miss I. (Croatia)
45 Makarova Miss E. (Russia)
23 Maleeva Miss M. (Bulgaria)
5 Martincova Miss E. (Czech Republic)
49 Martinez Miss C. (Spain)
35 Maruska Miss M. (Austria)
56 McNeil Miss L.M. (USA)
127 McQuillan Miss R. (Australia)
Meier Miss S. (Germany)
Melicharova Miss E. (Czech Republic)
116 Miyagi Miss N. (Japan)
Montalvo Miss L. (Argentina)
121 Morariu Miss C. (USA)
Muric Miss M. (Croatia)
47 Nagyova Miss H. (Slovakia)
77 Neiland Mrs L. (Latvia)
84 Nemeckova Miss L. (Czech Republic)
Nideffer Mrs R. (South Africa)
Noorlander Miss S. (Netherlands)
96 Novotna Miss J. (Czech Republic)
83 Olsza Miss A. (Poland)
42 Oremans Miss M. (Netherlands)
46 Panova Miss T. (Russia)
Park Miss S-H. (South Korea)
80 Paulus Miss B. (Austria)
Paz Miss M. (Argentina)
39 Perfetti Miss F. (Italy)
112 Pierce Miss M. (France)
106 Pitkowski Miss S. (France)
92 Pizzichini Miss G. (Italy)
Pleming Miss L. (Australia)
113 Po Miss K. (USA)
26 Pratt Miss N.J. (Australia)
95 Probst Miss W. (Germany)
24 Pullin Miss J.M. (Great Britain)
6 Raymond Miss L.M. (USA)
87 Richterova Miss L. (Czech Republic)
Rinaldi-Stunkel Mrs K.S. (USA)
60 Rittner Miss B. (Germany)
109 Ruano Pascual Miss V. (Spain)
57 Rubin Miss C. (USA)
67 Saeki Miss M. (Japan)
40 Sanchez Lorenzo Miss M. (Spain)
97 Sanchez Vicario Miss A. (Spain)
85 Sawamatsu Miss N. (Japan)
71 Schett Miss B. (Austria)
Schneider Miss C. (Germany)
123 Schnitzer Miss M. (Germany)
118 Schnyder Miss P. (Switzerland)
16 Schultz-McCarthy Mrs B. (Netherland)
128 Seles Miss M. (USA)
108 Serna Miss M. (Spain)
Shriver Miss P.H. (USA)
54 Siddall Miss S-A. (Great Britain)
59 Sidot Miss A-G. (France)
12 Simpson Miss R. (Canada)
86 Smith Miss S. (Great Britain)
Smylie Mrs P.D. (Australia)
48 Spirlea Miss I. (Romania)
25 Studenikova Miss K. (Slovakia)
104 Suarez Miss P. (Argentina)
73 Sugiyama Miss A. (Japan)
53 Sukova Miss H. (Czech Republic)
88 Tanasugarn Miss T. (Thailand)
Tarabini Miss P. (Argentina)
Tatarkova Miss E. (Ukraine)
115 Tauziat Miss N. (France)
122 Taylor Miss C. (Great Britain)
124 Testud Miss S. (France)
91 Torrens-Valero Miss C. (Spain)
75 Tu Miss M. (USA)
82 Van Lottum Miss N. (France)
111 Van Roost Mrs D. (Belgium)
20 Vento Miss M.A. (Venezuela)
Vildova Miss H. (Czech Republic)
Vis Miss C.M. (Netherlands)
Wagner Mrs E. (Germany)
Wainwright Miss A.M.H. (Great Britain)
55 Wang Miss S. (Taipeh)
Ward Miss J. (Great Britain)
107 Watanabe Miss J. (USA)
119 Wiesner Mrs J.K. (Austria)
38 Wild Miss L.M. (USA)
69 Williams Miss V. (USA)
98 Wood Miss C.J. (Great Britain)
Wood Miss J. (Great Britain)
117 Woodroffe Miss L.A. (Great Britain)
51 Yoshida Miss Y. (Japan)
27 Zrubakova Miss R. (Slovakia)
93 Zvereva Miss N. (Belarus)

GENTLEMEN

Adams D. (South Africa)
Albano P. (Argentina)
74 Alvarez E. (Spain)
109 Arazi H. (Morocco)
Arthurs W. (Australia)
Barnard M. (South Africa)
42 Baur P. (Germany)
32 Becker B. (Germany)
Behrens B. (USA)
Bergh R. (Sweden)
18 Bhupathi M. (India)
65 Bjorkman J. (Sweden)
7 Black B. (Zimbabwe)
Black W. (Zimbabwe)
108 Boetsch A. (France)
Braasch K. (Germany)
Brandi C. (Italy)
Broad N. (Great Britain)
111 Bryan S. (USA)
39 Burrieza O. (Spain)
73 Carlsen K. (Denmark)
8 Cash P. (Australia)
64 Chang M. (USA)
119 Charpentier M. (Argentina)
90 Clavet F. (Spain)
69 Clement A. (France)
Connell G. (Canada)
78 Courier J. (USA)
Couto E. (Portugal)
Cowan B. (Great Britain)
95 Craca M. (Germany)
Cunha-Silva J. (Portugal)
118 Damm M. (Czech Republic)
12 Davids H.J. (Netherlands)
Davis S.E. (USA)
De Jager J-L. (South Africa)
Delaitre O. (France)
83 Delgado J. (Great Britain)
94 Dewulf F. (Belgium)
Dilucia D. (USA)
85 Dosedel S. (Czech Republic)
114 Draper S. (Australia)
3 Dreekmann H. (Germany)
102 Duran S. (Spain)
Eagle J. (Australia)
Ekerot D. (Sweden)
105 Ellwood B. (Australia)
Eltingh J. (Netherlands)
Ferreira E. (South Africa)
113 Ferreira W. (South Africa)
121 Fetterlein F. (Denmark)
15 Filippini M. (Uruguay)
106 Flach D. (USA)
Fleurian J-P. (France)
Florent A. (Australia)
Forget G. (France)
Foster A.L. (Great Britain)
117 Frana J. (Argentina)
4 Fredriksson P. (Sweden)
20 Fromberg R. (Australia)
24 Furlan R. (Italy)
Galbraith P. (USA)
116 Gilbert R. (France)
79 Gimelstob J. (USA)
11 Godwin N. (South Africa)
104 Goellner M. (Germany)
84 Golmard J. (France)
31 Gorriz M. (Spain)
Grabb J. (USA)
Groen S. (Netherlands)
55 Gustafsson M. (Sweden)
88 Haarhuis P. (Netherlands)
26 Haas T. (Germany)
Haggard C. (South Africa)
Hand P.T. (Great Britain)
Haygarth B. (South Africa)
81 Henman T. (Great Britain)
126 Herrera L.E. (Mexico)
Hirszon S. (Croatia)
9 Holm H. (Sweden)
Holm N. (Sweden)
29 Hrbaty D. (Slovakia)
99 Huet S. (France)
128 Ivanisevic G. (Croatia)
Jensen L.B. (USA)
Jensen M. (USA)
30 Johansson T. (Sweden)
Johnson D. (USA)
Jones K. (USA)
33 Kafelnikov Y. (Russia)
60 Karbacher B. (Germany)
Keil M. (USA)
Kempers T. (Netherlands)
44 Kiefer N. (Germany)
Kilderry P. (Australia)
Kinnear K. (USA)
Kitinov A. (MacEdonia)
52 Knippschild J. (Germany)
Knowles M. (Bahamas)
Koenig R. (South Africa)
16 Korda P. (Czech Republic)
96 Krajicek R. (Netherlands)
Kratzmann A. (Australia)
Kronemann T. (USA)
28 Kroslak J. (Slovakia)
14 Kucera K. (Slovakia)
80 Kuerten G. (Brazil)
37 Kulti N. (Sweden)
89 Lapentti N. (Ecuador)
87 Lareau S. (Canada)
86 Larkham T. (Australia)
Lavergne R. (France)
Leach R. (USA)
72 Lee M. (Great Britain)
Macpherson D. (Australia)
MacPhie B. (USA)
34 Marin J. (Spain)
71 Marques N. (Portugal)
59 Martelli M. (Italy)
51 McGuire W. (USA)
48 Medvedev A. (Ukraine)
Melville S. (USA)
Messori F. (Italy)
Middleton T. (USA)
70 Milligan L. (Great Britain)
Mirnyi M. (Belarus)
Montana F. (USA)
Mota B. (Portugal)
112 Moya C. (Spain)
Muller G. (South Africa)
82 Nestor D. (Canada)
Nijssen T. (Netherlands)
125 Norman M. (Sweden)
Norval P. (South Africa)
Noteboom S. (Netherlands)
122 Novak J. (Czech Republic)
Nyborg P. (Sweden)
10 O'Brien A. (USA)
Olhovskiy A. (Russia)
62 Ondruska M. (South Africa)
Oosting M. (Netherlands)
Orsanic D. (Argentina)
68 Paes L. (India)
93 Pavel A. (Romania)
6 Pereira N. (Venezuela)
127 Pescariu D. (Romania)
27 Petchey M.R.J. (Great Britain)
97 Philippoussis M. (Australia)
Pimek L. (Belgium)
120 Pioline C. (France)
58 Radulescu A. (Germany)
49 Rafter P. (Australia)
Randall D. (USA)
107 Raoux G. (France)
110 Reneberg R.A. (USA)
101 Richardson A.L. (Great Britain)
91 Rikl D. (Czech Republic)
17 Rios M. (Chile)
13 Rosset M. (Switzerland)
123 Roux L. (France)
Rueb A. (USA)
98 Rusedski G. (Great Britain)
25 Ruud C. (Norway)
41 Salzenstein J. (USA)
1 Sampras P. (USA)
Sanchez E. (Spain)
36 Sanchez J. (Spain)
47 Santoro F. (France)
5 Sapsford D.E. (Great Britain)
45 Sargsian S. (Armenia)
61 Schalken S. (Netherlands)
23 Siemerink J. (Netherlands)
Simian S. (France)
38 Sinner M. (Germany)
Smith R. (Bahamas)
56 Spadea V. (USA)
50 Stafford G. (South Africa)
21 Stanoytchev O. (Bulgaria)
100 Stark J. (USA)
124 Steven B. (New Zealand)
77 Stich M. (Germany)
75 Stolle S. (Australia)
40 Stoltenberg J. (Australia)
Suk C. (Czech Republic)
Talbot B. (South Africa)
115 Tarango J. (USA)
35 Tebbutt M. (Australia)
2 Tillstrom M. (Sweden)
Tramacchi P. (Australia)
Trotman J.M. (Great Britain)
Ullyett K. (South Africa)
92 Vacek D. (Czech Republic)
Van Emburgh G. (USA)
53 Van Garsse C. (Belgium)
46 Van Herck J. (Belgium)
22 Van Lottum J. (Netherlands)
Van Rensburg C.J. (South Africa)
19 Van Scheppingen D. (Netherlands)
103 Viloca J. (Spain)
Vizner P. (Czech Republic)
57 Voinea A. (Romania)
43 Volkov A. (Russia)
Waite J. (USA)
54 Weal N. (Great Britain)
Wibier F. (Netherlands)
66 Wilkinson C. (Great Britain)
63 Woodbridge T.A. (Australia)
67 Woodforde M. (Australia)
76 Woodruff C. (USA)

GIRLS

11 Arrangoiz Miss P. (Mexico)
50 Bajin Miss S. (Canada)
48 Black Miss C. (Zimbabwe)
27 Bracun Miss I. (Croatia)
39 Braverman Miss B. (USA)
61 Callow Miss T. (Great Britain)
31 Castano Miss C. (Columbia)
51 Chevalier Miss K. (France)
9 Cho Miss Y-J. (South Korea)
6 Collin Miss H. (Great Britain)
58 Colosio Miss B. (Brazil)
19 Coombs Miss C. (Great Britain)
7 Danilidou Miss H. (Greece)
53 Dell'angelo Miss L. (Italy)
17 Dominjkovic Miss E. (Australia)
45 Dyrberg Miss E. (Denmark)
14 Elliott Miss K. (Great Britain)
60 Farr Miss H. (Great Britain)
3 Fujiwara Miss R. (Japan)
43 Grahame Miss A. (Australia)
2 Grandin Miss N. (South Africa)
28 Gubacsi Miss Z. (Hungary)
62 Henin Miss J. (Belgium)
35 Herbert Miss L. (Great Britain)
57 Inoue Miss M. (Japan)
12 Irvin Miss M. (USA)
20 Iversen Miss M. (Denmark)
13 Krstulovic Miss E. (Croatia)
59 Lastra Miss G. (USA)
29 Lydon Miss S. (Great Britain)
34 Matevzic Miss M. (Slovenia)
24 Morigami Miss A. (Japan)
44 Mouhtassine Miss B. (Morocco)
47 Niroj Miss M. (Thailand)
22 Osman Miss J. (Great Britain)
54 Palencia Miss P. (Mexico)
46 Pillay Miss A. (South Africa)
25 Popescu Miss C. (Canada)
49 Poutchek Miss T. (Belarus)
23 Prakusya Miss W. (Indonesia)
15 Rejniak Miss O. (Poland)
16 Rippner Miss A. (USA)
36 Rizzi Miss S. (France)
10 Sanchez Miss L. (France)
64 Sandu Miss R. (Romania)
41 Sebova Miss A. (Slovakia)
40 Selyutina Miss I. (Kazakstan)
21 Sequera Miss M. (Venezuela)
55 Singian Miss J.T. (USA)
8 Srebotnik Miss K. (Slovenia)
56 Stewart Miss B. (Australia)
33 Syssoeva Miss E. (Russia)
5 Taylor Miss S. (USA)
18 Teperberg Miss R. (Israel)
52 Tordoff Miss A. (Great Britain)
42 Turner Miss S. (Great Britain)
26 Urickova Miss S. (Slovakia)
30 Van Rooyen Miss L. (South Africa)
37 Visic Miss I. (Croatia)
4 Volekova Miss G. (Slovakia)
38 White Miss J. (Great Britain)
32 Woehr Miss J. (Germany)
1 Wood Miss L. (Great Britain)
63 Woodhouse Miss N.J. (Great Britain)

BOYS

4 Adaktusson J. (Sweden)
39 Aniola F. (Poland)
23 Babej F. (Slovakia)
6 Barnes A. (Great Britain)
22 Bates I.A. (Great Britain)
51 Belcher D. (Great Britain)
46 Beros I. (Croatia)
19 Cardinali F. (Argentina)
9 Cheng W. (Taipeh)
29 Chramosta L. (Czech Republic)
60 Christensen J. (Sweden)
63 Dent T. (USA)
47 Derapasko A. (Russia)
61 Dickson S. (Great Britain)
62 Duenas J. (Dominican Republic)
44 Dulko A. (Argentina)
1 Elsner D. (Germany)
7 Gnjatovic N. (Yugoslavia)
49 Gonzalez F. (Chile)
41 Gregorc M. (Slovenia)
45 Grolmus M. (Slovakia)
2 Haehnel J. (France)
53 Healey N. (Australia)
12 Hewitt L. (Australia)
10 Heyerdahl T. (Norway)
64 Horna L. (Peru)
13 Ilowski J. (Poland)
3 Ivanov-Smolenski K. (Russia)
16 Jeanpierre J. (France)
52 Jegede R. (Nigeria)
42 Karpenko O. (Ukraine)
Kiernan D. (Great Britain)
28 Kutanjac L. (Croatia)
36 Lee S-H. (South Korea)
40 Levant O. (France)
57 Lisnard J. (France)
14 Llodra M. (France)
35 Luzzi F. (Italy)
56 Malisse X. (Belgium)
17 Massu N. (Chile)
54 Messmer T. (Germany)
58 Mullins D. (Eire)
38 Nita R. (Romania)
50 Overholser N. (USA)
55 Papp Z. (Hungary)
34 Qureshi A. (Pakistan)
11 Ram A. (Israel)
59 Rizo R. (Mexico)
25 Rochus O. (Belgium)
26 Romero V. (Mexico)
20 Sciortino D. (Italy)
30 Sherwood D. (Great Britain)
31 Simoni A. (Brazil)
32 Srichaphan P. (Thailand)
27 Terachi T. (Japan)
37 Trotman J.M. (Great Britain)
15 Vaci B. (Hungary)
24 Vahaly B. (USA)
21 Van De Westhuizen J. (South Africa)
8 Vik R. (Czech Republic)
33 Whitehouse W. (South Africa)
18 Widhiyanto F. (Indonesia)
5 Zaher S. (Egypt)
43 Zewar M. (Egypt)
48 Ziv K. (Israel)

Bold figures denote position in Singles Draw

The winner becomes the holder, for the year only, of the CHALLENGE CUP presented by The All England Lawn Tennis and Croquet Club. The winner receives a silver replica of the Challenge Cup. A silver salver is presented to the runner-up and a bronze medal to each defeated semi-finalist.

First Round	Second Round	Third Round	Fourth Round	Quarter-Finals	Semi-Finals	Final
1. P.Sampras [1] ....(USA)	P.Sampras [1] 6/4 6/4 6/2					
2. M.Tillstrom ....(SWE)		P.Sampras [1]				
3. H.Dreekmann ....(GER)	H.Dreekmann 6/3 6/4 6/3	..............7/6(2) 7/5 7/5				
4. P.Fredriksson ....(SWE)			P.Sampras [1]			
(W) 5. D.E.Sapsford ....(GBR)	D.E.Sapsford ....3/6 6/2 7/6(5) 6/3		...........6/1 6/2 6/2			
(L) 6. N.Pereira ....(VEN)		B.Black				
7. B.Black ....(ZIM)	B.Black ....3/6 7/6(3) 6/4 6/4	............6/2 7/5 6/2				
(Q) 8. P.Cash ....(AUS)				P.Sampras [1]		
9. H.Holm ....(SWE)	A.O'Brien ....7/6(5) 6/4 7/6(4)			.......6/4 6/3 6/7(8) 6/7(1) 6/4		
10. A.O'Brien ....(USA)		A.O'Brien				
11. N.Godwin ....(RSA)	N.Godwin ....7/5 7/6(2) 6/3	......6/3 6/3 6/7(6) 7/6(5)				
(Q) 12. H.J.Davids ....(NED)			P.Korda [16]			
13. M.Rosset ....(SUI)	M.Rosset 7/5 6/2 6/3		.....6/3 4/6 6/3 6/7(1) 6/4			
14. K.Kucera ....(SVK)		P.Korda [16]				
15. M.Filippini ....(URU)	P.Korda [16] ....4/6 7/6(4) 6/1 6/4	.........6/3 6/0 7/6(8)				
16. P.Korda [16] ....(CZE)					P.Sampras [1]	
17. M.Rios [9] ....(CHI)	M.Rios [9] 6/4 6/4 6/3				...6/1 6/7(5) 6/1 6/4	
18. M.Bhupathi ....(IND)		M.Rios [9]				
(Q) 19. D.Van Scheppingen ....(NED)	D.Van Scheppingen 5/7 6/4 3/6 6/1 6/4	......6/2 6/3 6/7(1) 7/6(7)				
20. R.Fromberg ....(AUS)			M.Rios [9]			
21. O.Stanoytchev ....(BUL)	J.Van Lottum 3/6 2/6 6/3 6/1 6/3		.......7/6(4) 6/3 6/7(5) 6/4			
(Q) 22. J.Van Lottum ....(NED)		J.Van Lottum				
23. J.Siemerink ....(NED)	R.Furlan ......6/7(5) 6/7(4) 6/4 6/4 6/4	............6/3 6/3 6/3				
24. R.Furlan ....(ITA)				B.Becker [8]		
25. C.Ruud ....(NOR)	T.Haas 6/2 6/1 6/2			.......6/2 6/2 7/6(5)		
26. T.Haas ....(GER)		M.R.J.Petchey				
(W) 27. M.R.J.Petchey ....(GBR)	M.R.J.Petchey 6/1 6/2 6/1	...........7/6(4) 6/4 6/2				
28. J.Kroslak ....(SVK)			B.Becker [8]			
29. D.Hrbaty ....(SVK)	T.Johansson 7/5 6/3 6/1		.......6/3 6/3 6/2			
30. T.Johansson ....(SWE)		B.Becker [8]				
31. M.Gorriz ....(ESP)	B.Becker [8] 6/3 6/2 6/3	............6/1 6/4 6/4				
32. B.Becker [8] ....(GER)						P.Sampras [1]
33. Y.Kafelnikov [3] ....(RUS)	Y.Kafelnikov [3] 6/4 6/2 6/0					6/2 6/1 7/6(3)
34. J.Marin ....(ESP)		Y.Kafelnikov [3]				
(Q) 35. M.Tebbutt ....(AUS)	J.Sanchez 3/6 4/6 6/4 7/5 14/12	.........6/2 4/6 6/3 6/4				
36. J.Sanchez ....(ESP)			Y.Kafelnikov [3]			
37. N.Kulti ....(SWE)	N.Kulti ....7/6(3) 6/2 6/3		.....6/3 7/6(4) 4/6 6/3			
38. M.Sinner ....(GER)		J.Stoltenberg				
(Q) 39. O.Burrieza ....(ESP)	J.Stoltenberg 6/3 6/4 6/3	.........6/2 3/6 6/2 6/3				
40. J.Stoltenberg ....(AUS)				N.Kiefer		
(Q) 41. J.Salzenstein ....(USA)	P.Baur ......7/6(5) 3/6 3/6 6/4 9/7			.........6/2 7/5 2/6 6/1		
(Q) 42. P.Baur ....(GER)		N.Kiefer				
43. A.Volkov ....(RUS)	N.Kiefer 6/4 6/4 6/2	........7/5 7/6(2) 6/1				
44. N.Kiefer ....(GER)			N.Kiefer			
45. S.Sargsian ....(ARM)	S.Sargsian ....7/6(4) 6/2 6/4		.....6/4 6/2 6/7(2) 6/4			
46. J.Van Herck ....(BEL)		A.Medvedev [13]				
47. F.Santoro ....(FRA)	A.Medvedev [13] 6/2 6/3 6/4	.........6/1 6/4 7/5				
48. A.Medvedev [13] ....(UKR)				N.Kiefer		
49. P.Rafter [12] ....(AUS)	P.Rafter [12] 2/6 4/6 6/3 6/2 6/2			.........6/2 7/5 2/6 6/1		
50. G.Stafford ....(RSA)		P.Rafter [12]				
(Q) 51. W.McGuire ....(USA)	J.Knippschild 6/4 6/4 6/4	.........6/3 4/6 6/3 6/0				
52. J.Knippschild ....(GER)			P.Rafter [12]			
(Q) 53. C.Van Garsse ....(BEL)	C.Van Garsse ....6/1 7/6(4) 7/6(3)		.......7/5 6/4 4/6 6/3			
(W) 54. N.Weal ....(GBR)		C.Van Garsse				
55. M.Gustafsson ....(SWE)	M.Gustafsson 6/2 6/1 6/3	............6/4 6/4 6/1				
56. V.Spadea ....(USA)				T.A.Woodbridge		
57. A.Voinea ....(ROM)	A.Radulescu ....7/6(5) 3/6 6/1 3/6 6/4			.......6/7(2) 6/4 7/6(6) 6/3		
58. A.Radulescu ....(GER)		A.Radulescu				
59. M.Martelli ....(ITA)	M.Martelli 6/4 6/3 6/1	............6/3 7/5 6/4				
60. B.Karbacher ....(GER)			T.A.Woodbridge			
61. S.Schalken ....(NED)	M.Ondruska ....3/6 7/5 6/0 0/1 Ret'd		.....6/4 6/4 6/4			
62. M.Ondruska ....(RSA)		T.A.Woodbridge				
63. T.A.Woodbridge ....(AUS)	T.A.Woodbridge ....7/6(5) 3/6 6/2 3/6 8/6	.......7/5 6/1 7/6(3)				
64. M.Chang [5] ....(USA)					T.A.Woodbridge	
65. J.Bjorkman [17] ....(SWE)	C.Wilkinson .....7/6(5) 0/6 5/7 6/3 6/4				7/6(7) 2/6 6/0 6/4	
(W) 66. C.Wilkinson ....(GBR)		M.Woodforde				
67. M.Woodforde ....(AUS)	M.Woodforde 6/3 7/5 6/4	..........5/7 5/7 6/2 6/4 6/1				
68. L.Paes ....(IND)			M.Woodforde			
(Q) 69. A.Clement ....(FRA)	A.Clement ....2/6 7/6(1) 7/5 6/2		........6/2 6/3 6/3			
(W) 70. L.Milligan ....(GBR)		A.Clement				
71. N.Marques ....(POR)	M.Lee 7/5 6/3 6/3	.........4/6 6/2 6/3 6/4				
(W) 72. M.Lee ....(GBR)				M.Stich		
73. K.Carlsen ....(DEN)	E.Alvarez ......6/7(4) 3/6 6/4 6/1 6/2			..........6/4 6/7(3) 6/3 7/5		
74. E.Alvarez ....(ESP)		S.Stolle				
75. S.Stolle ....(AUS)	S.Stolle 6/2 6/2 6/4	...........6/4 6/4 6/4				
76. C.Woodruff ....(USA)			M.Stich			
77. M.Stich ....(GER)	M.Stich ....7/6(0) 7/5 7/6(2)		.....6/3 6/7(5) 6/2 7/6(4)			
78. J.Courier ....(USA)		M.Stich				
79. J.Gimelstob ....(USA)	J.Gimelstob 6/3 6/4 6/4 1/6 6/4	...........7/5 6/1 6/1				
80. G.Kuerten [11] ....(BRA)						P.Sampras [1]
81. T.Henman [14] ....(GBR)	T.Henman [14] ....7/6(11) 6/1 6/4					6/4 6/2 6/4
82. D.Nestor ....(CAN)		T.Henman [14]				
(W) 83. J.Delgado ....(GBR)	J.Golmard ......6/4 6/2 6/7(4) 6/2	.........7/6(4) 6/3 6/2				
84. J.Golmard ....(FRA)			T.Henman [14]			
85. S.Dosedel ....(CZE)	T.Larkham ....6/7(3) 6/3 6/4 7/5		.......6/7(7) 6/3 6/2 4/6 14/12			
(Q) 86. T.Larkham ....(AUS)		P.Haarhuis				
87. S.Lareau ....(CAN)	P.Haarhuis ....6/1 6/2 7/6(5)	.........3/6 6/3 6/1 6/2				
88. P.Haarhuis ....(NED)				T.Henman [14]		
89. N.Lapentti ....(ECU)	F.Clavet 7/5 6/1 6/3			......7/6(7) 6/7(7) 7/6(5) 6/4		
90. F.Clavet ....(ESP)		D.Rikl				
(Q) 91. D.Rikl ....(CZE)	D.Rikl 6/1 6/3 6/3	...........6/4 7/6(5) 6/4				
92. D.Vacek ....(CZE)			R.Krajicek [4]			
93. A.Pavel ....(ROM)	A.Pavel 6/1 4/6 2/6 6/2 6/3		.....6/4 6/3 7/5			
94. F.Dewulf ....(BEL)		R.Krajicek [4]				
95. M.Craca ....(GER)	R.Krajicek [4] ....7/6(5) 6/2 6/4	........3/6 6/4 6/7(4) 6/3 6/3				
96. R.Krajicek [4] ....(NED)					C.Pioline	
97. M.Philippoussis [7] ......(AUS)	G.Rusedski ....7/6(6) 7/6(6) 6/3				6/7(2) 6/2 6/1 5/7 6/4	
98. G.Rusedski ....(GBR)		G.Rusedski				
(L) 99. S.Huet ....(FRA)	J.Stark ......7/6(5) 6/7(5) 6/3 2/6 6/3	..........4/6 6/7(9) 6/4 6/3 11/9				
100. J.Stark ....(USA)			G.Rusedski			
(W)101. A.L.Richardson ....(GBR)	A.L.Richardson ....7/6(5) 6/3 6/3		........6/3 6/4 6/4			
(Q)102. S.Duran ....(ESP)		A.L.Richardson				
103. J.Viloca ....(ESP)	J.Viloca ......7/5 4/6 7/6(5) 7/6(5)	.........6/3 3/6 6/4 2/6 6/2				
104. M.Goellner ....(GER)				G.Rusedski		
(L) 105. B.Ellwood ....(AUS)	D.Flach ....6/1 7/6(4) 3/6 6/4			.........7/6(2) 6/4 7/6(4)		
106. D.Flach ....(USA)		G.Raoux				
107. G.Raoux ....(FRA)	G.Raoux 6/3 6/4 6/1	..........6/3 6/7(5) 6/3 6/1				
108. A.Boetsch ....(FRA)			R.A.Reneberg			
109. H.Arazi ....(MAR)	R.A.Reneberg ....7/6(6) 6/4 7/6(5)		.......7/5 6/7(4) 7/6(7) 6/3			
110. R.A.Reneberg ....(USA)		R.A.Reneberg				
(L) 111. S.Bryan ....(USA)	C.Moya [10] ....7/6(1) 6/3 4/6 6/2	............6/4 6/3 6/3				
112. C.Moya [10] ....(ESP)						
113. W.Ferreira [15] ....(RSA)	W.Ferreira [15] ....6/7(5) 3/6 6/4 6/0 7/5				C.Pioline	
114. S.Draper ....(AUS)		W.Ferreira [15]				6/4 4/6 6/4 6/3
115. J.Tarango ....(USA)	R.Gilbert ....3/6 7/5 7/6(0) 6/4	.........7/6(5) 4/6 6/3 3/6 9/7				
(Q) 116. R.Gilbert ....(FRA)			C.Pioline			
117. J.Frana ....(ARG)	J.Frana ....6/7(5) 6/4 6/3		......6/4 6/3 6/3			
118. M.Damm ....(CZE)		C.Pioline				
119. M.Charpentier ....(ARG)	C.Pioline 5/7 3/7 5/7 6/2	..............w/o				
120. C.Pioline ....(FRA)				C.Pioline		
121. F.Fetterlein ....(DEN)	F.Fetterlein ....4/6 3/6 6/4 7/6(3) 6/4			.........3/6 6/3 6/4 7/5		
122. J.Novak ....(CZE)		B.Steven				
123. L.Roux ....(FRA)	B.Steven ....6/2 6/2 7/6(0)	..........4/6 7/5 6/3 6/2				
124. B.Steven ....(NZL)			B.Steven			
125. M.Norman ....(SWE)	M.Norman ....7/6(6) 6/1 6/4		.....6/7(5) 6/2 6/3 6/2			
(Q) 126. L.E Herrera ....(MEX)		M.Norman				
127. D.Pescariu ....(ROM)	G.Ivanisevic [2] 6/1 6/3 6/4	..........6/3 2/6 7/6(4) 4/6 14/12				
128. G.Ivanisevic [2] ....(CRO)						

Heavy type denotes seeded players. The figure in brackets against names denotes the order in which they have been seeded. (W) = Wild card. (Q) = Qualifier. (L) = Lucky loser.

The matches are the best of five sets

THE GENTLEMEN'S DOUBLES CHAMPIONSHIP

Holders: T.A. Woodbridge and M. Woodforde

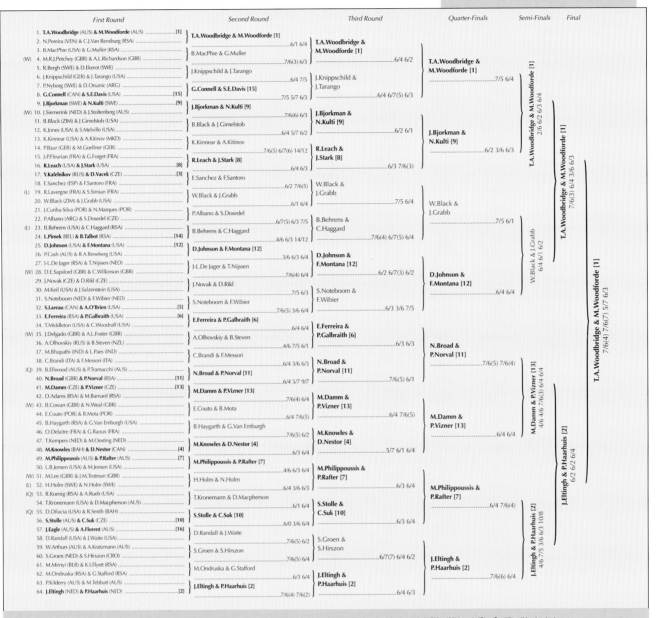

	First Round	Second Round	Third Round	Quarter-Finals	Semi-Finals	Final

1. T.A.Woodbridge (AUS) & M.Woodforde (AUS) ....[1]
2. N.Pereira (VEN) & C.J.Van Rensburg (RSA)
3. B.MacPhie (USA) & G.Muller (RSA)
(W) 4. M.R.J.Petchey (GBR) & A.L.Richardson (GBR)
5. R.Bergh (SWE) & D.Ekerot (SWE)
6. J.Knippschild (GER) & J.Tarango (USA)
7. P.Nyborg (SWE) & D.Orsanic (ARG)
8. G.Connell (CAN) & S.E.Davis (USA) ....[15]
9. J.Bjorkman (SWE) & N.Kulti (SWE) ....[9]
(W) 10. J.Siemerink (NED) & J.Stoltenberg (AUS)
11. B.Black (ZIM) & J.Gimelstob (USA)
12. K.Jones (USA) & S.Melville (USA)
13. K.Kinnear (USA) & A.Kitinov (MKD)
14. P.Baur (GER) & M.Goellner (GER)
15. J-P.Fleurian (FRA) & G.Forget (FRA)
16. R.Leach (USA) & J.Stark (USA) ....[8]
17. Y.Kafelnikov (RUS) & D.Vacek (CZE) ....[3]
18. E.Sanchez (ESP) & F.Santoro (FRA)
(L) 19. R.Lavergne (FRA) & S.Simian (FRA)
20. W.Black (ZIM) & J.J.Grabb (USA)
21. J.Cunha-Silva (POR) & N.Marques (POR)
22. P.Albano (ARG) & S.Dosedel (CZE)
(L) 23. B.Behrens (USA) & C.Haggard (RSA)
24. L.Pimek (BEL) & B.Talbot (RSA) ....[14]
25. D.Johnson (USA) & F.Montana (USA) ....[12]
26. P.Cash (AUS) & R.A.Reneberg (USA)
27. J-L.De Jager (RSA) & T.Nijssen (NED)
(W) 28. D.E.Sapsford (GBR) & C.Wilkinson (GBR)
29. J.Novak (CZE) & D.Rikl (CZE)
30. M.Keil (USA) & J.Salzenstein (USA)
31. S.Noteboom (NED) & F.Wibier (NED)
32. S.Lareau (CAN) & A.O'Brien (USA) ....[5]
33. E.Ferreira (RSA) & P.Galbraith (USA) ....[6]
34. T.Middleton (USA) & C.Woodruff (USA)
(W) 35. J.Delgado (GBR) & A.L.Foster (GBR)
36. A.Olhovskiy (RUS) & B.Steven (NZL)
37. M.Bhupathi (IND) & L.Paes (IND)
38. C.Brandi (ITA) & F.Messori (ITA)
(Q) 39. B.Ellwood (AUS) & P.Tramacchi (AUS)
40. N.Broad (GBR) & P.Norval (RSA) ....[11]
41. M.Damm (CZE) & P.Vizner (CZE) ....[13]
42. D.Adams (RSA) & M.Barnard (RSA)
(W) 43. B.Cowan (GBR) & N.Weal (GBR)
44. E.Couto (POR) & B.Mota (POR)
45. B.Haygarth (RSA) & G.Van Emburgh (USA)
46. O.Delaitre (FRA) & G.Raoux (FRA)
47. T.Kempers (NED) & M.Oosting (NED)
48. M.Knowles (BAH) & D.Nestor (CAN) ....[4]
49. M.Philippoussis (AUS) & P.Rafter (AUS) ....[7]
50. L.B.Jensen (USA) & M.Jensen (USA)
(W) 51. M.Lee (GBR) & J.M.Trotman (GBR)
(L) 52. H.Holm (SWE) & N.Holm (SWE)
(Q) 53. R.Koenig (RSA) & A.Rueb (USA)
54. T.Kronemann (USA) & D.Macpherson (AUS)
(Q) 55. D.Dilucia (USA) & R.Smith (BAH)
56. S.Stolle (AUS) & C.Suk (CZE) ....[10]
57. J.Eagle (AUS) & A.Florent (AUS) ....[16]
58. D.Randall (USA) & J.Waite (USA)
59. W.Arthurs (AUS) & A.Kratzmann (AUS)
60. S.Groen (NED) & S.Hirszon (CRO)
61. M.Mirnyi (BLR) & K.Ullyett (RSA)
62. M.Ondruska (RSA) & G.Stafford (RSA)
63. P.Kilderry (AUS) & M.Tebbutt (AUS)
64. J.Eltingh (NED) & P.Haarhuis (NED) ....[2]

Second Round:
- T.A.Woodbridge & M.Woodforde [1] ... 6/1 6/4
- B.MacPhie & G.Muller ... 7/6(3) 6/3
- J.Knippschild & J.Tarango ... 6/4 7/5
- G.Connell & S.E.Davis [15] ... 7/5 5/7 6/3
- J.Bjorkman & N.Kulti [9] ... 7/6(6) 6/3
- B.Black & J.Gimelstob ... 6/4 5/7 6/2
- K.Kinnear & A.Kitinov ... 7/6(5) 6/7(6) 14/12
- R.Leach & J.Stark [8] ... 6/4 6/3
- E.Sanchez & F.Santoro ... 6/2 7/6(5)
- W.Black & J.Grabb ... 6/1 6/4
- P.Albano & S.Dosedel ... 6/7(5) 6/3 7/5
- B.Behrens & C.Haggard ... 4/6 6/4 14/12
- D.Johnson & F.Montana [12] ... 3/6 6/3 6/4
- J-L.De Jager & T.Nijssen ... 7/6(4) 6/4
- J.Novak & D.Rikl ... 7/5 6/3
- S.Noteboom & F.Wibier ... 7/6(5) 3/6 6/4
- E.Ferreira & P.Galbraith [6] ... 6/4 6/4
- A.Olhovskiy & B.Steven ... 4/6 7/5 6/1
- C.Brandi & F.Messori ... 6/4 3/6 6/3
- N.Broad & P.Norval [11] ... 6/4 5/7 9/7
- M.Damm & P.Vizner [13] ... 7/6(4) 6/4
- E.Couto & B.Mota ... 6/4 7/6(5)
- B.Haygarth & G.Van Emburgh ... 7/6(5) 6/2
- M.Knowles & D.Nestor [4] ... 6/3 6/4
- M.Philippoussis & P.Rafter [7] ... 4/6 6/3 6/4
- H.Holm & N.Holm ... 6/4 3/6 6/3
- T.Kronemann & D.Macpherson ... 6/1 6/4
- S.Stolle & C.Suk [10] ... 6/0 3/6 6/4
- D.Randall & J.Waite ... 7/6(5) 6/2
- S.Groen & S.Hirszon ... 7/6(5) 6/2
- M.Ondruska & G.Stafford ... 6/3 6/4
- J.Eltingh & P.Haarhuis [2] ... 7/6(4) 7/6(2)

Third Round:
- T.A.Woodbridge & M.Woodforde [1] ... 6/4 6/2
- J.Knippschild & J.Tarango ... 6/4 6/7(5) 6/3
- J.Bjorkman & N.Kulti [9] ... 6/2 6/1
- R.Leach & J.Stark [8] ... 6/3 7/6(3)
- W.Black & J.Grabb ... 7/5 6/4
- B.Behrens & C.Haggard ... 7/6(4) 6/7(5) 6/4
- D.Johnson & F.Montana [12] ... 6/2 6/7(3) 6/2
- S.Noteboom & F.Wibier ... 6/3 3/6 7/5
- E.Ferreira & P.Galbraith [6] ... 6/3 6/3
- N.Broad & P.Norval [11] ... 7/6(5) 6/1
- M.Damm & P.Vizner [13] ... 6/4 7/6(5)
- M.Knowles & D.Nestor [4] ... 5/7 6/1 6/4
- M.Philippoussis & P.Rafter [7] ... 6/3 6/4
- S.Stolle & C.Suk [10] ... 6/3 6/4
- S.Groen & S.Hirszon ... 6/7(7) 6/4 6/2
- J.Eltingh & P.Haarhuis [2] ... 6/4 6/3

Quarter-Finals:
- T.A.Woodbridge & M.Woodforde [1] ... 7/5 6/4
- J.Bjorkman & N.Kulti [9] ... 6/2 3/6 6/3
- W.Black & J.Grabb ... 7/5 6/1
- D.Johnson & F.Montana [12] ... 6/4 6/4
- N.Broad & P.Norval [11] ... 7/6(5) 7/6(4)
- M.Damm & P.Vizner [13] ... 6/4 6/4
- M.Philippoussis & P.Rafter [7] ... 6/4 7/6(4)
- J.Eltingh & P.Haarhuis [2] ... 7/6(6) 6/4

Semi-Finals:
- T.A.Woodbridge & M.Woodforde [1] ... 2/6 6/2 6/3 6/4
- W.Black & J.Grabb ... 6/4 6/1 6/2
- M.Damm & P.Vizner [13] ... 4/6 4/6 7/6(3) 6/4 6/4
- J.Eltingh & P.Haarhuis [2] ... 4/6 7/5 3/6 10/8

Final:
- T.A.Woodbridge & M.Woodforde [1] ... 7/6(4) 7/6(7) 5/7 6/3

Winner: T.A.Woodbridge & M.Woodforde [1] ... 7/6(3) 6/4 3/6 6/3

Heavy type denotes seeded players. The figure in brackets against names denotes the order in which they have been seeded. (W) = Wild card. (Q) = Qualifier. (L) = Lucky loser.

The matches are the best of three sets up to the quarter-finals, best of five sets thereafter

---

THE 45 AND OVER GENTLEMEN'S INVITATION DOUBLES

Holders: J.G. Alexander and P.C. Dent

	First Round	Second Round	Semi-Finals	Final

1. J.G.Alexander (AUS) & P.C.Dent (AUS) ....[1]
2. M.Cox (GBR) & M.Santana (ESP)
3. J.W.Feaver (GBR) & R.Taylor (GBR)
4. J.D.Newcombe (AUS) & A.D.Roche (AUS)
5. I.Nastase (ROM) & T.S.Okker (NED) ....[3]
6. O.K.Davidson (AUS) & E.C.Drysdale (RSA)
7. K.R.Rosewall (AUS) & F.S.Stolle (AUS)
8. R.C.Lutz (USA) & R.Tanner (USA)
9. J.Fillol (CHI) & R.L.Stockton (USA)
10. J.Kodes (CZE) & A.Metreveli (RUS)
11. N.A.Fraser (AUS) & A.J.Stone (AUS)
12. R.A.J.Hewitt (RSA) & F.D.McMillan (RSA) ....[4]
13. R.L.Case (AUS) & G.Masters (AUS)
14. B.E.Gottfried (USA) & T.R.Gullikson (USA)
15. T.W.Gorman (USA) & S.R.Smith (USA)
16. M.C.Riessen (USA) & S.E.Stewart (USA) ....[2]

Second Round:
- J.G.Alexander & P.C.Dent [1] ... 6/0 6/3
- J.D.Newcombe & A.D.Roche ... 7/6(2) 7/6(4)
- O.K.Davidson & E.C.Drysdale ... 4/6 6/3 6/4
- R.C.Lutz & R.Tanner ... 6/1 6/4
- J.Fillol & R.L.Stockton ... 6/2 6/1
- N.A.Fraser & A.J.Stone ... 6/3 6/2
- B.E.Gottfried & T.R.Gullikson ... 6/4 6/2
- M.C.Riessen & S.E.Stewart [2] ... 6/1 7/5

Semi-Finals:
- J.G.Alexander & P.C.Dent [1] ... 6/4 6/4
- O.K.Davidson & E.C.Drysdale ... 6/3 6/4
- J.Fillol & R.L.Stockton ... 6/1 6/3
- M.C.Riessen & S.E.Stewart [2] ... w/o

Final:
- O.K.Davidson & E.C.Drysdale ... 7/6(2) 6/4
- J.Fillol & R.L.Stockton ... 7/6(4) 6/4

Winner: J.Fillol & R.L.Stockton ... 6/1 6/2

Heavy type denotes seeded players. The figure in brackets against names denotes the order in which they have been seeded.

The matches are the best of three sets

The winner becomes the holder, for the year only, of the CHALLENGE TROPHY presented by The All England Lawn Tennis and Croquet Club. The winner receives a silver replica of the Trophy. A silver salver is presented to the runner-up and a bronze medal to each defeated semi-finalist.

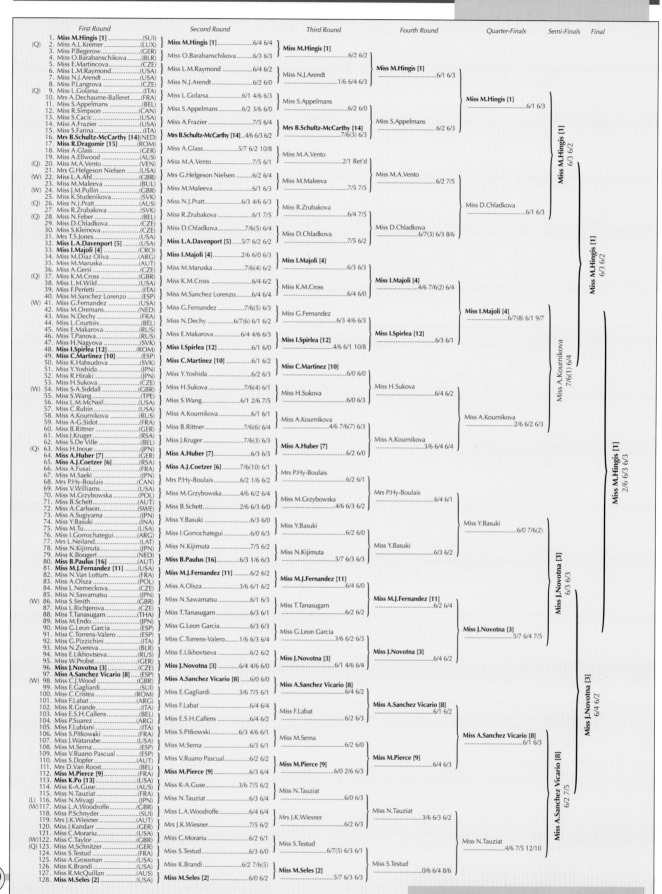

First Round	Second Round	Third Round	Fourth Round	Quarter-Finals	Semi-Finals	Final

1. Miss M.Hingis [1] ....(SUI)
(Q) 2. Miss A.L.Kremer ....(LUX)
3. Miss P.Begerow ....(GER)
4. Miss O.Barabanschikova .....(BLR)
5. Miss E.Martincova ....(CZE)
6. Miss L.M.Raymond ....(USA)
7. Miss N.J.Arendt ....(USA)
8. Miss P.Langrova ....(CZE)
(Q) 9. Miss L.Golarsa ....(ITA)
10. Mrs A.Dechaume-Balleret ....(FRA)
11. Miss S.Appelmans ....(BEL)
12. Miss R.Simpson ....(CAN)
13. Miss S.Cacic ....(USA)
14. Miss A.Frazier ....(USA)
15. Miss S.Farina ....(ITA)
16. Mrs B.Schultz-McCarthy [14](NED)
17. Miss R.Dragomir [15] ....(ROM)
18. Miss A.Glass ....(GER)
19. Miss A.Ellwood ....(AUS)
(Q) 20. Miss M.A.Vento ....(VEN)
21. Mrs G.Helgeson Nielsen .....(USA)
(W) 22. Miss L.A.Ahl ....(GBR)
23. Miss M.Maleeva ....(BUL)
(W) 24. Miss J.M.Pullin ....(GBR)
25. Miss K.Studenikova ....(SVK)
(Q) 26. Miss N.J.Pratt ....(AUS)
27. Miss R.Zrubakova ....(SVK)
(Q) 28. Miss N.Feber ....(BEL)
29. Miss D.Chladkova ....(CZE)
30. Miss S.Kleinova ....(CZE)
31. Mrs T.S.Jones ....(USA)
32. Miss L.A.Davenport [5] ....(USA)
33. Miss I.Majoli [4] ....(CRO)
34. Miss M.Diaz Oliva ....(ARG)
35. Miss M.Maruska ....(AUT)
36. Miss A.Gersi ....(CZE)
(Q) 37. Miss K.M.Cross ....(GBR)
38. Miss L.M.Wild ....(USA)
39. Miss F.Perfetti ....(ITA)
40. Miss M.Sanchez Lorenzo ......(ESP)
(W) 41. Miss G.Fernandez ....(USA)
42. Miss M.Oremans ....(NED)
43. Miss N.Dechy ....(FRA)
44. Miss L.Courtois ....(BEL)
45. Miss E.Makarova ....(RUS)
46. Miss T.Panova ....(RUS)
47. Miss H.Nagyova ....(SVK)
48. Miss I.Spirlea [12] ....(ROM)
49. Miss C.Martinez [10] ....(ESP)
50. Miss K.Habsudova ....(SVK)
51. Miss Y.Yoshida ....(JPN)
52. Miss R.Hiraki ....(JPN)
53. Miss H.Sukova ....(CZE)
(W) 54. Miss S-A.Siddall ....(GBR)
55. Miss S.Wang ....(TPE)
56. Miss L.M.McNeil ....(USA)
57. Miss C.Rubin ....(USA)
58. Miss A.Kournikova ....(RUS)
59. Miss A-G.Sidot ....(FRA)
60. Miss B.Rittner ....(GER)
61. Miss J.Kruger ....(RSA)
62. Miss S.De Ville ....(BEL)
(Q) 63. Miss H.Inoue ....(JPN)
64. Miss A.Huber [7] ....(GER)
65. Miss A.J.Coetzer [6] ....(RSA)
66. Miss A.Fusai ....(FRA)
67. Miss M.Saeki ....(JPN)
68. Mrs P.Hy-Boulais ....(CAN)
69. Miss V.Williams ....(USA)
70. Miss M.Grzybowska ....(POL)
71. Miss B.Schett ....(AUT)
72. Miss A.Carlsson ....(SWE)
73. Miss A.Sugiyama ....(JPN)
74. Miss Y.Basuki ....(INA)
75. Miss M.Tu ....(USA)
76. Miss I.Gorrochategui ....(ARG)
77. Mrs N.Neiland ....(LAT)
78. Miss N.Kijimuta ....(JPN)
79. Miss K.Boogert ....(NED)
80. Miss B.Paulus [16] ....(AUT)
81. Miss M.J.Fernandez [11] ....(USA)
82. Miss N.Van Lottum ....(FRA)
83. Miss A.Olsza ....(POL)
84. Miss L.Nemeckova ....(CZE)
85. Miss N.Sawamatsu ....(JPN)
(W) 86. Miss S.Smith ....(GBR)
87. Miss L.Richterova ....(CZE)
88. Miss T.Tanasugarn ....(THA)
89. Miss M.Endo ....(JPN)
90. Miss G.Leon Garcia ....(ESP)
91. Miss C.Torrens-Valero ....(ESP)
92. Miss G.Pizzichini ....(ITA)
93. Miss N.Zvereva ....(BLR)
94. Miss E.Likhovtseva ....(RUS)
95. Miss W.Probst ....(GER)
96. Miss J.Novotna [3] ....(CZE)
97. Miss A.Sanchez Vicario [8] ....(ESP)
(W) 98. Miss C.J.Wood ....(GBR)
99. Miss E.Gagliardi ....(SUI)
100. Miss C.Cristea ....(ROM)
101. Miss F.Labat ....(ARG)
102. Miss R.Grande ....(ITA)
103. Miss E.S.H.Callens ....(BEL)
104. Miss P.Suarez ....(ARG)
105. Miss F.Lubiani ....(ITA)
106. Miss S.Pitkowski ....(FRA)
107. Miss J.Watanabe ....(JPN)
108. Miss M.Serna ....(ESP)
109. Miss V.Ruano Pascual ....(ESP)
110. Miss S.Dopfer ....(AUT)
111. Mrs D.Van Roost ....(BEL)
112. Miss M.Pierce [9] ....(FRA)
113. Miss K.Po [13] ....(USA)
114. Miss K-A.Guse ....(AUS)
115. Miss N.Tauziat ....(FRA)
(L) 116. Miss N.Miyagi ....(JPN)
(W)117. Miss L.A.Woodroffe ....(GBR)
118. Miss P.Schnyder ....(SUI)
119. Miss J.K.Wiesner ....(AUT)
120. Miss J.Kandarr ....(GER)
121. Miss C.Morariu ....(USA)
(W)122. Miss C.Taylor ....(GBR)
(Q)123. Miss K.Schnitzer ....(GER)
124. Miss S.Testud ....(FRA)
125. Miss A.Grossman ....(USA)
126. Miss K.Brandi ....(USA)
127. Miss R.McQuillan ....(AUS)
128. Miss M.Seles [2] ....(USA)

Second Round

Miss M.Hingis [1] 6/4 6/4
Miss O.Barabanschikova 6/3 6/3
Miss L.M.Raymond 6/4 6/2
Miss N.J.Arendt 6/2 6/0
Miss L.Golarsa 6/1 4/6 6/3
Miss S.Appelmans 6/2 3/6 6/0
Miss A.Frazier 7/5 6/4
Mrs B.Schultz-McCarthy [14]...4/6 6/3 6/2
Miss A.Glass 5/7 6/2 10/8
Miss M.A.Vento 7/5 6/1
Mrs G.Helgeson Nielsen 6/2 6/4
Miss M.Maleeva 6/1 6/3
Miss N.J.Pratt 6/3 4/6 6/2
Miss R.Zrubakova 6/1 7/5
Miss D.Chladkova ....7/6(5) 6/4
Miss L.A.Davenport [5] 5/7 6/2 6/2
Miss I.Majoli [4] 2/6 6/0 6/3
Miss M.Maruska ....7/6(4) 6/2
Miss K.M.Cross 6/4 6/2
Miss M.Sanchez Lorenzo..........6/4 6/4
Miss G.Fernandez ....7/6(5) 6/3
Miss N.Dechy ....6/7(6) 6/1 6/2
Miss E.Makarova 6/4 4/6 6/3
Miss I.Spirlea [12] 6/1 6/0
Miss C.Martinez [10] 6/1 6/2
Miss Y.Yoshida 6/2 6/3
Miss H.Sukova ....7/6(4) 6/1
Miss S.Wang 6/1 2/6 7/5
Miss A.Kournikova 6/1 6/1
Miss B.Rittner ....7/6(6) 6/4
Miss J.Kruger ....7/6(3) 6/3
Miss A.Huber [7] 6/3 6/3
Miss A.J.Coetzer [6] ....7/6(10) 6/1
Mrs P.Hy-Boulais 6/2 1/6 6/2
Miss M.Grzybowska 4/6 6/2 6/4
Miss B.Schett 2/6 6/3 6/0
Miss Y.Basuki 6/3 6/0
Miss I.Gorrochategui 6/0 6/3
Miss N.Kijimuta 7/5 6/2
Miss B.Paulus [16] 6/3 1/6 6/3
Miss M.J.Fernandez [11] 6/2 6/2
Miss A.Olsza 3/6 6/1 6/2
Miss N.Sawamatsu 6/1 6/3
Miss T.Tanasugarn 6/3 6/1
Miss G.Leon Garcia 6/3 6/3
Miss C.Torrens-Valero 1/6 6/3 6/4
Miss E.Likhovtseva 6/2 6/2
Miss J.Novotna [3] 6/4 4/6 6/0
Miss A.Sanchez Vicario [8] 6/0 6/0
Miss E.Gagliardi 3/6 7/5 6/1
Miss F.Labat 6/4 6/4
Miss E.S.H.Callens 6/4 6/2
Miss S.Pitkowski 6/3 4/6 6/1
Miss M.Serna 6/3 6/1
Miss V.Ruano Pascual 6/2 6/2
Miss M.Pierce [9] 6/3 6/4
Miss K-A.Guse 3/6 7/5 6/2
Miss N.Tauziat 6/3 6/4
Miss L.A.Woodroffe 6/4 6/4
Mrs J.K.Wiesner 7/5 6/2
Miss C.Morariu 6/2 6/1
Miss S.Testud 6/3 6/0
Miss K.Brandi ....6/2 7/6(5)
Miss M.Seles [2] 6/0 6/2

Third Round

Miss M.Hingis [1] 6/2 6/2
Miss N.J.Arendt 1/6 6/4 6/3
Miss S.Appelmans 6/2 6/0
Mrs B.Schultz-McCarthy [14]...7/6(3) 6/3
Miss M.A.Vento ....2/1 Ret'd
Miss M.Maleeva 7/5 7/5
Miss R.Zrubakova 6/4 7/5
Miss D.Chladkova 7/5 6/2
Miss I.Majoli [4] 6/3 6/3
Miss K.M.Cross 6/4 6/0
Miss G.Fernandez 6/3 4/6 6/3
Miss I.Spirlea [12] 4/6 6/1 10/8
Miss C.Martinez [10] 6/0 6/0
Miss H.Sukova 6/0 6/3
Miss A.Kournikova ....4/6 7/6(7) 6/3
Miss A.Huber [7] 6/2 6/0
Mrs P.Hy-Boulais 6/2 6/1
Miss M.Grzybowska 4/6 6/3 6/2
Miss Y.Basuki 6/2 6/0
Miss N.Kijimuta 5/7 6/3 6/4
Miss M.J.Fernandez [11] 6/4 6/0
Miss T.Tanasugarn 6/2 6/2
Miss G.Leon Garcia 3/6 6/2 6/2
Miss J.Novotna [3] 6/1 4/6 6/0
Miss A.Sanchez Vicario [8] 6/4 6/2
Miss F.Labat 6/2 6/0
Miss M.Serna 6/2 6/0
Miss M.Pierce [9] 6/0 2/6 6/3
Miss N.Tauziat 6/0 6/3
Mrs J.K.Wiesner 6/2 6/3
Miss S.Testud ....6/7(5) 6/3 6/1
Miss M.Seles [2] 5/7 6/3 6/3

Fourth Round

Miss M.Hingis [1] 6/1 6/3
Miss S.Appelmans 6/2 6/3
Miss M.A.Vento 6/2 7/5
Miss D.Chladkova ....6/7(3) 6/3 8/6
Miss I.Majoli [4] ....4/6 7/6(2) 6/4
Miss I.Spirlea [12] 6/3 6/1
Miss H.Sukova 6/4 6/2
Miss A.Kournikova 3/6 6/4 6/4
Mrs P.Hy-Boulais 6/4 6/1
Miss Y.Basuki 6/3 6/2
Miss M.J.Fernandez [11] 7/6 6/4
Miss J.Novotna [3] 6/4 6/2
Miss A.Sanchez Vicario [8] 6/1 6/2
Miss M.Pierce [9] 6/4 6/3
Miss N.Tauziat 3/6 6/3 6/2
Miss S.Testud 0/6 6/4 8/6

Quarter-Finals

Miss M.Hingis [1] 6/1 6/3
Miss D.Chladkova 6/1 6/3
Miss I.Majoli [4] ....6/7(8) 6/1 9/7
Miss A.Kournikova 2/6 6/2 6/3
Miss Y.Basuki ....6/0 7/6(2)
Miss J.Novotna [3] 5/7 6/4 7/5
Miss A.Sanchez Vicario [8] 6/1 6/3
Miss N.Tauziat 4/6 7/5 12/10

Semi-Finals

Miss M.Hingis [1]
6/3 6/2

Miss A.Kournikova
7/6(1) 6/4

Miss M.Hingis [1]
6/3 6/2

Miss J.Novotna [3]
6/4 6/2

Miss A.Sanchez Vicario [8]
6/2 7/5

Final

Miss M.Hingis [1]
6/3 6/3

Miss J.Novotna [3]
2/6 6/3 6/3

Miss M.Hingis [1]
2/6 6/3 6/3

THE LADIES' DOUBLES CHAMPIONSHIP

Holders: Miss M. Hingis and Miss H. Sukova

First Round	Second Round	Third Round	Quarter-Finals	Semi-Finals	Final

1. Miss G.Fernandez (USA) & Miss N.Zvereva (BLR) ....[1]
(W) 2. Miss O.Barabanschikova (BLR) & Miss S.Smith (GBR)
3. Miss K.Freye (GER) & Miss S.Noorlander (NED)
4. Mrs P.Hy-Boulais (CAN) & Miss K.Studenikova (SVK)
5. Miss C.G.Barclay (AUS) & Miss C.J.Wood (GBR)
6. Miss S.Farina (ITA) & Miss B.Schett (AUT)
(W) 7. Miss J.M.Pullin (GBR) & Miss L.A.Woodroffe (GBR)
8. Miss K.Boogert (NED) & Miss I.Spirlea (ROM) ....[16]
9. Miss K.M.Adams (USA) & Miss L.M.McNeil (USA) ....[9]
10. Miss V.Ruano Pascual (ESP) & Miss P.Suarez (ARG)
11. Miss B.Rittner (GER) & Mrs D.Van Roost (BEL)
12. Miss A.Ellwood (AUS) & Miss R.McQuillan (AUS)
13. Miss C.Cristea (ROM) & Miss M.Grzybowska (POL)
14. Miss A.Carlsson (SWE) & Miss F.Perfetti (ITA)
15. Miss M.de Swardt (RSA) & Miss L.Horn (RSA)
16. Miss M.J.Fernandez (USA) & Miss L.M.Raymond (USA) ....[5]
17. Miss L.A.Davenport (USA) & Miss J.Novotna (CZE) ....[3]
18. Miss T.Krizan (SLO) & Miss N.Van Lottum (FRA)
19. Miss D.A.Graham (USA) & Mrs K.Kunce (AUS)
(L) 20. Miss J.Lutrova (RUS) & Miss J.Wood (GBR)
(W) 21. Miss S-A.Siddall (GBR) & Miss A.M.H.Wainwright (GBR)
22. Miss P.Langrova (CZE) & Miss R.Zrubakova (SVK)
23. Miss M.Paz (ARG) & Miss A-G.Sidot (FRA)
24. Miss A.Fusai (FRA) & Miss R.Grande (ITA) ....[13]
25. Miss S.Appelmans (BEL) & Miss M.Oremans (NED) ....[12]
26. Miss R.Dragomir (ROM) & Miss I.Majoli (CRO)
27. Miss D.J.Jones (AUS) & Miss T.Tanasugarn (THA)
28. Mrs A.Dechaume-Balleret (FRA) & Miss S.Testud (FRA)
29. Miss L.Garrone (ITA) & Miss G.Pizzichini (ITA)
30. Miss A.Grossman (USA) & Miss K.Habsudova (SVK)
31. Miss S.Jeyaseelan (CAN) & Miss R.Simpson (CAN)
32. Miss Y.Basuki (INA) & Miss C.M.Vis (NED) ....[8]
33. Miss C.Martinez (ESP) & Miss P.Tarabini (ARG) ....[7]
34. Miss E.S.H.Callens (BEL) & Mrs G.Helgeson Nielsen (USA)
35. Miss R.Nideffer (RSA) & Mrs K.S.Rinaldi-Stunkel (USA)
36. Miss A.Huber (GER) & Miss M.Seles (USA)
(Q) 37. Miss E.Brioukhovets (RUS) & Miss E.Tatarkova (UKR)
38. Miss T.S.Jones (USA) & Miss M.Muric (CRO)
39. Miss R.Hiraki (JPN) & Miss F.Labat (ARG)
40. Miss A.Frazier (USA) & Miss K.Po (USA) ....[14]
41. Miss N.Tauziat (FRA) & Miss L.M.Wild (USA) ....[10]
42. Miss A.J.Coetzer (RSA) & Miss M.Pierce (FRA)
43. Miss J.Lee (USA) & Miss A.Olsza (POL)
44. Miss L.Golarsa (ITA) & Miss P.Schnyder (SUI)
45. Miss S.Meier (GER) & Miss L.Nemeckova (CZE)
46. Miss O.Lugina (UKR) & Mrs E.Wagner (GER)
47. Miss L.Montalvo (ARG) & Miss H.Nagyova (SVK)
48. Mrs L.Neiland (LAT) & Miss H.Sukova (CZE) ....[4]
49. Miss N.J.Arendt (USA) & Miss M.M.Bollegraf (NED) ....[6]
(W) 50. Miss C.Taylor (GBR) & Miss J.Ward (GBR)
51. Miss S-H.Park (KOR) & Miss S.Wang (TPE)
(Q) 52. Miss V.Lake (GBR) & Miss L.Pleming (AUS)
53. Miss P.H.Shriver (USA) & Mrs P.D.Smylie (AUS)
54. Miss A.Kournikova (RUS) & Miss E.Likhovtseva (RUS)
55. Miss V.Csurgo (HUN) & Miss C.Schneider (GER)
56. Miss N.Kijimuta (JPN) & Miss N.Miyagi (JPN) ....[11]
57. Miss C.Rubin (USA) & Mrs B.Schultz-McCarthy (NED) ....[15]
58. Miss W.Probst (GER) & Miss A.Sugiyama (JPN)
59. Miss M.Saeki (JPN) & Miss Y.Yoshida (JPN)
60. Miss E.R.De Lone (USA) & Miss N.J.Pratt (AUS)
61. Miss R.Bobkova (CZE) & Miss E.Melicharova (CZE)
62. Miss K-A.Guse (AUS) & Miss C.Morariu (USA)
63. Miss E.Martincova (CZE) & Miss H.Vildova (CZE)
64. Miss M.Hingis (SUI) & Miss A.Sanchez Vicario (ESP) ....[2]

Second Round

Miss G.Fernandez & Miss N.Zvereva [1] 6/2 6/2
Miss K.Freye & Miss S.Noorlander .... 7/6(5) 4/6 6/2
Miss C.G.Barclay & Miss C.J.Wood 6/4 6/3
Miss K.Boogert & Miss I.Spirlea [16] 6/3 6/2
Miss K.M.Adams & Miss L.M.McNeil [9] .... 7/6(3) 6/3
Miss B.Rittner & Mrs D.Van Roost 4/6 6/1 6/1
Miss C.Cristea & Miss M.Grzybowska 7/5 6/4
Miss M.J.Fernandez & Miss L.M.Raymond [5] 6/2 6/1
Miss L.A.Davenport & Miss J.Novotna [3] 6/0 6/2
Miss D.A.Graham & Mrs K.Kunce 6/4 6/1
Miss S-A.Siddall & Miss A.M.H.Wainwright 6/3 6/2
Miss A.Fusai & Miss R.Grande [13] 6/3 6/0
Miss S.Appelmans & Miss M.Oremans [12] .... w/o
Mrs A.Dechaume-Balleret & Miss S.Testud .... 6/2 7/6(3)
Miss L.Garrone & Miss G.Pizzichini 6/2 6/4
Miss Y.Basuki & Miss C.M.Vis [8] 6/4 6/2
Miss E.S.H.Callens & Mrs G.Helgeson Nielsen 6/4 7/5
Miss A.Huber & Miss M.Seles 7/5 6/3
Mrs T.S.Jones & Miss M.Muric 6/3 6/1
Miss A.Frazier & Miss K.Po [14] 7/5 6/3
Miss N.Tauziat & Miss L.M.Wild [10] 6/1 1/6 10/8
Miss L.Golarsa & Miss P.Schnyder 7/5 6/3
Miss O.Lugina & Mrs E.Wagner 6/4 4/6 6/4
Mrs L.Neiland & Miss H.Sukova [4] 3/6 6/1 6/4
Miss N.J.Arendt & Miss M.M.Bollegraf [6] 6/4 6/4
Miss S-H.Park & Miss S.Wang 6/4 6/4
Miss A.Kournikova & Miss E.Likhovtseva 3/6 7/5 9/7
Miss N.Kijimuta & Miss N.Miyagi [11] 6/4 6/3
Miss C.Rubin & Mrs B.Schultz-McCarthy [15] 6/1 7/5
Miss M.Saeki & Miss Y.Yoshida .... 6/7(1) 7/5 6/4
Miss K-A.Guse & Miss C.Morariu .... 6/7(5) 7/6(4) 6/1
Miss M.Hingis & Miss A.Sanchez Vicario [2] 6/2 6/3

Third Round

Miss G.Fernandez & Miss N.Zvereva [1] 6/0 6/2
Miss C.G.Barclay & Miss C.J.Wood .... 4/6 7/6(5) 6/4
Miss K.M.Adams & Miss L.M.McNeil [9] 6/3 1/6 6/4
Miss M.J.Fernandez & Miss L.M.Raymond [5] 6/3 6/0
Miss L.A.Davenport & Miss J.Novotna [3] 6/1 6/2
Miss A.Fusai & Miss R.Grande [13] 6/3 6/4
Miss S.Appelmans & Miss M.Oremans [12] 6/4 6/3
Miss Y.Basuki & Miss C.M.Vis [8] 5/7 6/4 6/2
Miss E.S.H.Callens & Mrs G.Helgeson Nielsen 6/2 6/4
Miss A.Frazier & Miss K.Po [14] 6/2 6/3
Miss N.Tauziat & Miss L.M.Wild [10] .... 6/7(5) 7/6(4) 6/3
Miss L.Neiland & Miss H.Sukova [4] 6/3 6/2
Miss N.J.Arendt & Miss M.M.Bollegraf [6] 6/2 6/0
Miss N.Kijimuta & Miss N.Miyagi [11] 4/6 6/2 7/5
Miss C.Rubin & Mrs B.Schultz-McCarthy [15] .... 7/6(5) 6/4
Miss M.Hingis & Miss A.Sanchez Vicario [2] 6/3 6/3

Quarter-Finals

Miss G.Fernandez & Miss N.Zvereva [1] 7/5 7/5
Miss M.J.Fernandez & Miss L.M.Raymond [5] .... 6/1 7/6(1)
Miss L.A.Davenport & Miss J.Novotna [3] 6/1 6/1
Miss S.Appelmans & Miss M.Oremans [12] 7/5 6/1
Miss E.S.H.Callens & Mrs G.Helgeson Nielsen .... 7/6(4) 6/4
Mrs L.Neiland & Miss H.Sukova [4] 6/4 6/4
Miss N.J.Arendt & Miss M.M.Bollegraf [6] 6/2 3/6 6/1
Miss M.Hingis & Miss A.Sanchez Vicario [2] .... 7/6(12) 6/7(6) 13/11

Semi-Finals

Miss G.Fernandez & Miss N.Zvereva [1] 5/7 6/4 6/4
Miss S.Appelmans & Miss M.Oremans [12] .... w/o
Mrs L.Neiland & Miss H.Sukova [4] 6/4 6/4
Miss N.J.Arendt & Miss M.M.Bollegraf [6] 6/4 5/7 6/2

Final

Miss G.Fernandez & Miss N.Zvereva [1] 6/1 6/2
Miss N.J.Arendt & Miss M.M.Bollegraf [6] 6/2 3/6 6/1
Miss G.Fernandez & Miss N.Zvereva [1] .... 7/6(4) 6/4

The winners become the holders, for the year only, of the CHALLENGE CUP presented by the family of the late Mr S.H. SMITH. The winners receive silver replicas of the Challenge Cup. A silver salver is presented to each of the runners-up and a bronze medal to each defeated semi-finalist.

Holders: C. Suk and Miss H. Sukova

First Round	Second Round	Third Round	Quarter-Finals	Semi-Finals	Final
1. G.Connell (CAN) & Miss L.A.Davenport (USA) ....[1]	G.Connell & Miss L.A.Davenport [1]	G.Connell & Miss L.A.Davenport [1]			
2. T.Kempers (NED) & Miss N.Van Lottum (FRA)	...................4/6 6/2 6/2		G.Connell & Miss L.A.Davenport [1]		
3. J.Waite (USA) & Miss M.Muric (CRO)		......................6/3 6/3			
4. D.Orsanic (ARG) & Miss F.Labat (ARG)	D.Orsanic & Miss F.Labat				
5. S.Noteboom (NED) & Miss S.Jeyaseelan (CAN)	....................6/4 7/6(6)	T.Middleton & Miss L.M.McNeil			
6. T.Middleton (USA) & Miss L.M.McNeil (USA)	T.Middleton & Miss L.M.McNeil			G.Connell & Miss L.A.Davenport [1]	
7. M.Mirnyi (BLR) & Miss E.Likhovtseva (RUS)	...................7/6(4) 7/5	......................7/6(5) 6/4		...................4/6 7/6(2) 6/4	
8. J.Eagle (AUS) & Miss C.M.Vis (NED) ....[9]	M.Mirnyi & Miss E.Likhovtseva				
9. M.Bhupathi (IND) & Miss R.Hiraki (JPN) ....[15]	...................7/6(3) 6/4	M.Bhupathi & Miss R.Hiraki [15]			
(W) 10. C.J.Van Rensburg (RSA) & Miss V.Williams (USA)	M.Bhupathi & Miss R.Hiraki [15]				
11. F.Messori (ITA) & Miss F.Perfetti (ITA)	...................6/7(4) 6/3 6/2		R.Leach & Miss M.M.Bollegraf [5]		
12. S.E.Davis (USA) & Miss P.Tarabini (ARG)	F.Messori & Miss F.Perfetti	......................3/6 7/5 6/3			
(W) 13. M.R.J.Petchey (GBR) & Miss C.J.Wood (GBR)	...................6/4 6/4				
14. E.Sanchez (ESP) & Miss A.Sanchez Vicario (ESP)	M.R.J.Petchey & Miss C.J.Wood	R.Leach & Miss M.M.Bollegraf [5]		G.Connell & Miss L.A.Davenport [1]	
15. R.Smith (BAH) & Miss A.Frazier (USA)	...................4/6 Ret'd			6/4 6/4	
16. R.Leach (USA) & Miss M.M.Bollegraf (NED) ....[5]	R.Leach & Miss M.M.Bollegraf [5]	......................7/6(4) 6/3	R.Leach & Miss M.M.Bollegraf [5]		
17. C.Suk (CZE) & Miss H.Sukova (CZE) ....[4]	...................6/1 2/6 6/2		......................6/3 5/7 6/4		
18. T.Kronemann (USA) & Mrs K.S.Rinaldi-Stunkel (USA)	C.Suk & Miss H.Sukova [4]	C.Suk & Miss H.Sukova [4]			
19. M.Jensen (USA) & Mrs B.Schultz-McCarthy (NED)	...................6/1 7/5				
20. J.Gimelstob (USA) & Miss C.Rubin (USA)	J.Gimelstob & Miss C.Rubin	......................7/6(2) 6/1			
21. P.Norval (RSA) & Miss L.Horn (RSA)	...................7/5 6/7(5) 6/1				
22. K.Kinnear (USA) & Miss N.Miyagi (JPN)	K.Kinnear & Miss N.Miyagi	K.Kinnear & Miss N.Miyagi			
23. A.Florent (AUS) & Miss C.G.Barclay (AUS)	...................7/6(1) 6/3		C.Suk & Miss H.Sukova [4]		
24. L.B.Jensen (USA) & Miss K.M.Adams (USA) ....[13]	L.B.Jensen & Miss K.M.Adams [13]	......................7/5 6/4	......................6/2 7/5		
25. L.Pimek (BEL) & Miss S.Appelmans (BEL) ....[11]	...................6/7(6) 6/1 13/11				
26. T.Nijssen (NED) & Miss Y.Basuki (INA)	T.Nijssen & Miss Y.Basuki	T.Nijssen & Miss Y.Basuki		C.Suk & Miss H.Sukova [4]	
27. M.Keil (USA) & Mrs G.Helgeson Nielsen (USA)	...................7/5 4/6 6/1			6/1 0/6 6/4	
28. P.Kilderry (AUS) & Miss S.Testud (FRA)	M.Keil & Mrs G.Helgeson Nielsen	......................6/3 6/4			
29. G.Raoux (FRA) & Miss L.Golarsa (ITA)	...................4/6 6/0 6/3		T.Nijssen & Miss Y.Basuki		
30. B.Talbot (RSA) & Mrs D.Van Roost (BEL)	G.Raoux & Miss L.Golarsa	D.Adams & Miss A.Fusai [7]	......................6/4 7/5		
31. K.Ullyett (RSA) & Mrs R.Nideffer (RSA)	...................6/3 7/6(3)				
32. D.Adams (RSA) & Miss A.Fusai (FRA) ....[7]	D.Adams & Miss A.Fusai [7]	......................6/3 6/4			
33. M.Knowles (BAH) & Miss A.Kournikova (RUS) ....[8]	...................6/7(2) 6/4 6/2				
34. S.Melville (USA) & Miss N.J.Pratt (AUS)	M.Knowles & Miss A.Kournikova [8]	L.Paes & Miss R.Dragomir			
(W) 35. C.Wilkinson (GBR) & Miss S.Smith (GBR)	...................6/4 7/5				
36. L.Paes (IND) & Miss R.Dragomir (ROM)	L.Paes & Miss R.Dragomir	......................w/o	L.Paes & Miss R.Dragomir		
37. M.Barnard (RSA) & Miss K.Boogert (NED)	...................4/6 6/3 6/1		......................5/7 6/3 6/4		
38. G.Van Emburgh (USA) & Miss E.Melicharova (CZE)	M.Barnard & Miss K.Boogert	M.Barnard & Miss K.Boogert			
39. D.Macpherson (AUS) & Miss R.McQuillan (AUS)	...................6/2 7/6(2)				
40. A.O'Brien (USA) & Miss C.Morariu (USA) ....[16]	A.O'Brien & Miss C.Morariu [16]	......................2/6 6/4 6/3		A.Olhovskiy & Mrs L.Neiland [3]	
41. P.Albano (ARG) & Miss M.Paz (ARG) ....[14]	...................6/7(4) 7/6(4) 13/11			6/3 7/6(5)	
42. A.Kratzmann (AUS) & Miss K-A.Guse (AUS)	P.Albano & Miss M.Paz [14]	W.Arthurs & Miss T.Krizan			
43. W.Arthurs (AUS) & Miss T.Krizan (SLO)	...................6/2 6/4				
44. A.Kitinov (MKD) & Miss A.Olsza (POL)	W.Arthurs & Miss T.Krizan	......................6/4 6/2	A.Olhovskiy & Mrs L.Neiland [3]		
45. R.Bergh (SWE) & Mrs P.Hy-Boulais (CAN)	...................7/5 1/6 11/9		......................6/2 7/6(4)		
46. P.Nyborg (SWE) & Miss A.Carlsson (SWE)	P.Nyborg & Miss A.Carlsson	A.Olhovskiy & Mrs L.Neiland [3]			
47. D.Ekerot (SWE) & Miss K.Pleming (AUS)	...................7/5 5/7 6/4				
48. A.Olhovskiy (RUS) & Mrs L.Neiland (LAT) ....[3]	A.Olhovskiy & Mrs L.Neiland [3]	......................7/5 6/3			
49. S.Stolle (AUS) & Miss M.J.Fernandez (USA) ....[6]	...................7/6(4) 6/1			A.Olhovskiy & Mrs L.Neiland [3]	
50. C.Brandi (ITA) & Mrs A.Dechaume-Balleret (FRA)	S.Stolle & Miss M.J.Fernandez [6]	N.Broad & Miss M.de Swardt		7/6(7) 4/6 6/3	
51. N.Broad (GBR) & Miss M.de Swardt (RSA)	...................7/6(4) 3/6 7/5				
52. D.Randall (USA) & Miss D.J.Jones (AUS)	N.Broad & Miss M.de Swardt	......................6/3 3/6 6/3	N.Broad & Miss M.de Swardt		
53. S.Groen (NED) & Miss H.Vildova (CZE)	...................7/5 6/4		......................7/5 6/3		
(W) 54. D.E.Sapsford (GBR) & Miss S-A.Siddall (GBR)	D.E.Sapsford & Miss S-A.Siddall	D.E.Sapsford & Miss S-A.Siddall			
55. H.J.Davids (NED) & Miss M.Oremans (NED)	...................7/5 7/5				
56. D.Johnson (USA) & Miss L.M.Wild (USA) ....[10]	D.Johnson & Miss L.M.Wild [10]	......................6/2 6/3			
57. J.Grabb (USA) & Miss D.A.Graham (USA) ....[12]	...................6/3 6/4			N.Broad & Miss M.de Swardt	
58. K.Braasch (GER) & Miss B.Rittner (GER)	K.Braasch & Miss B.Rittner	K.Braasch & Miss B.Rittner		5/7 7/6/3 6/4	
59. K.Jones (USA) & Mrs K.Kunce (AUS)	...................4/6 7/5 15/13				
60. B.Haygarth (RSA) & Mrs T.S.Jones (USA)	K.Jones & Mrs K.Kunce	......................6/2 5/7 6/4	J-L.De Jager & Miss M.Hingis		
61. P.T.Hand (GBR) & Miss V.Lake (GBR)	...................6/4 6/3		......................6/4 6/3		
62. J-L.De Jager (RSA) & Miss M.Hingis (SUI)	J-L.De Jager & Miss M.Hingis	J-L.De Jager & Miss M.Hingis			
63. W.Black (ZIM) & Miss A.Grossman (USA)	...................6/1 6/3				
64. P.Galbraith (USA) & Miss L.M.Raymond (USA) ....[2]	P.Galbraith & Miss L.M.Raymond [2]	......................6/4 0/6 10/8			
	...................4/6 6/3 7/5				

Final winners (right column):

C.Suk & Miss H.Sukova [4]
4/6 6/3 6/4

C.Suk & Miss H.Sukova [4]
3/6 6/2 6/3

A.Olhovskiy & Mrs L.Neiland [3]

Holders: W. Fibak and T. Wilkison

The winners become the holders, for the year only, of a Cup presented by The All England Lawn Tennis and Croquet Club. The winners receive miniature silver salvers. A silver medal is presented to each of the runners-up.

GROUP A

Pair	v	Match 1	Match 2	Match 3	Wins	Losses
P. Slozil (CZE) and T. Smid (CZE)	v	G.W. Donnelly (USA) and D. Visser (RSA) 4/6 6/3 1/6	C. Dowdeswell (GBR) and C.J. Mottram (GBR) 7/5 6/3	H. Pfister (USA) and L. Shiras (USA) 7/6(5) 3/6 6/3	2	1
G.W. Donnelly (USA) and D. Visser (RSA)	v	**P. Slozil (CZE) and T. Smid (CZE)** 6/4 3/6 6/1	H. Pfister (USA) and L. Shiras (USA) 7/5 6/4	C. Dowdeswell (GBR) and C.J. Mottram (GBR) 6/3 3/6 6/4	3	0
H. Pfister (USA) and L. Shiras (USA)	v	C. Dowdeswell (GBR) and C.J. Mottram (GBR) 6/1 6/7(3) 10/8	G.W. Donnelly (USA) and D. Visser (RSA) 5/7 4/6	**P. Slozil (CZE) and T. Smid (CZE)** 6/7(5) 6/3 3/6	1	2
C. Dowdeswell (GBR) and C.J. Mottram (GBR)	v	H. Pfister (USA) and L. Shiras (USA) 1/6 7/6(3) 8/10	**P. Slozil (CZE) and T. Smid (CZE)** 5/7 3/6	G.W. Donnelly (USA) and D. Visser (RSA) 3/6 6/3 4/6	0	3

GROUP B

Pair	v	Match 1	Match 2	Match 3	Wins	Losses
M.J. Bates (GBR) and R. Krishnan (IND)	v	A. Amritraj (IND) and V. Amritraj (IND) 6/2 5/7 6/4	A.A. Mayer (USA) and G. Mayer (USA) 7/6 6/2	M.R. Edmondson (AUS) and R.J. Frawley (AUS) 6/2 6/2	3	0
A. Amritraj (IND) and V. Amritraj (IND)	v	**M.J. Bates (GBR) and R. Krishnan (IND)** 2/6 7/5 4/6	M.R. Edmondson (AUS) and R.J. Frawley (AUS) 7/5 7/6(5)	A.A. Mayer (USA) and G. Mayer (USA) 1/6 6/4 4/6	1	2
M.R. Edmondson (AUS) and R.J. Frawley (AUS)	v	A.A. Mayer (USA) and G. Mayer (USA) 1/6 3/6	A. Amritraj (IND) and V. Amritraj (IND) 5/7 6/7(5)	**M.J. Bates (GBR) and R. Krishnan (IND)** 2/6 2/6	0	3
A.A. Mayer (USA) and G. Mayer (USA)	v	M.R. Edmondson (AUS) and R.J. Frawley (AUS) 6/1 6/3	**M.J. Bates (GBR) and R. Krishnan (IND)** 6/7 2/6	A. Amritraj (IND) and V. Amritraj (IND) 6/1 4/6 6/4	2	1

GROUP C

Pair	v	Match 1	Match 2	Match 3	Wins	Losses
J.B. Fitzgerald (AUS) and A. Jarryd (SWE)	v	A.M. Jarrett (GBR) and J.R. Smith (GBR) 4/6 6/1 6/2	H. Guenthardt (SUI) and B. Taroczy (HUN) 6/3 7/6(6)	M. Bahrami (IRN) and P. Dupre (USA) 6/2 4/6 6/1	3	0
A.M. Jarrett (GBR) and J.R. Smith (GBR)	v	**J.B. Fitzgerald (AUS) and A. Jarryd (SWE)** 6/4 1/6 2/6	M. Bahrami (IRN) and P. Dupre (USA) 7/6(3) 6/1	H. Guenthardt (SUI) and B. Taroczy (HUN) 7/6(2) 7/6(3)	2	1
M. Bahrami (IRN) and P. Dupre (USA)	v	H. Guenthardt (SUI) and B. Taroczy (HUN) 6/7(2) 1/6	A.M. Jarrett (GBR) and J.R. Smith (GBR) 6/7(3) 1/6	**J.B. Fitzgerald (AUS) and A. Jarryd (SWE)** 2/6 6/4 1/6	0	3
H. Guenthardt (SUI) and B. Taroczy (HUN)	v	M. Bahrami (IRN) and P. Dupre (USA) 7/6(2) 6/1	**J.B. Fitzgerald (AUS) and A. Jarryd (SWE)** 3/6 6/7(6)	A.M. Jarrett (GBR) and J.R. Smith (GBR) 6/7(2) 6/7(3)	1	2

GROUP D

Pair	v	Match 1	Match 2	Match 3	Wins	Losses
W. Fibak (POL) and T. Wilkison (USA)	v	P.B. McNamara (AUS) and P.F. McNamee (AUS) 6/3 6/4	B. Gilbert (USA) and T. Mayotte (USA) 6/3 3/6 2/6	K. Curren (USA) and J.C. Kriek (USA) 6/3 3/6 2/6	2	1
P.B. McNamara (AUS) and P.F. McNamee (AUS)	v	**W. Fibak (POL) and T. Wilkison (USA)** 3/6 4/6	K. Curren (USA) and J.C. Kriek (USA) 3/6 4/6	B. Gilbert (USA) and T. Mayotte (USA) 1/6 6/3 6/4	1	2
K. Curren (USA) and J.C. Kriek (USA)	v	B. Gilbert (USA) and T. Mayotte (USA) 6/4 6/2	P.B. McNamara (AUS) and P.F. McNamee (AUS) 6/3 6/4	**W. Fibak (POL) and T. Wilkison (USA)** 3/6 6/3 6/2	3	0
B. Gilbert (USA) and T. Mayotte (USA)	v	K. Curren (USA) and J.C. Kriek (USA) 4/6 2/6	**W. Fibak (POL) and T. Wilkison (USA)** 3/6 4/6	P.B. McNamara (AUS) and P.F. McNamee (AUS) 6/1 3/6 4/6	0	3

SEMI-FINAL

- G.W. Donnelly (USA) and D. Visser (RSA)
- M.J. Bates (GBR) and R. Krishnan (IND) — **M.J. Bates (GBR) and R. Krishnan (IND)** 3/6 6/1 7/5
- J.B. Fitzgerald (AUS) and A. Jarryd (SWE)
- K. Curren (USA) and J.C. Kriek (USA) — **K. Curren (USA) and J.C. Kriek (USA)** 6/3 7/6(7)

FINAL

- M.J. Bates (GBR) and R. Krishnan (IND) 6/4 6/4

This event is played on a 'round robin' basis. Sixteen invited pairs are divided into four groups and each pair in each group plays the others. The pairs winning most matches are the winners of their respective groups and play semi-final and final rounds as indicated above.

If matches should be equal in any group, the head-to-head result between the two pairs with the same number of wins determines the winning pair of the group.

Heavy type denotes seeded players.

The matches are the best of three sets

The winners become the holders, for the year only, of a Cup presented by The All England Lawn Tennis and Croquet Club. The winners receive miniature Cups. A silver medal is presented to each of the runners-up.

Holders: Miss J.M. Durie and Miss A.E. Smith

GROUP A				WINS	LOSSES	FINAL
Miss J.M. Durie (GBR) and Miss A.E. Smith (USA) V	Miss R. Casals (USA) and Miss B. F. Stove (NED) 6/2 6/2	Mrs R. Nideffer (RSA) and Miss S. Walsh (USA) 6/1 6/3	Miss H. Mandlikova (AUS) and Miss J.C. Russell (USA) 6/0 6/1	3	0	Miss J.M. Durie (GBR) and Miss A.E. Smith (USA)
Miss R. Casals (USA) and Miss B. F. Stove (NED) V	Miss J.M. Durie (GBR) and Miss A.E. Smith (USA) 2/6 2/6	Miss H. Mandlikova (AUS) and Miss J.C. Russell (USA) 6/7(6) 2/6	Mrs R. Nideffer (RSA) and Miss S. Walsh (USA) w/o	1	2	
Miss H. Mandlikova (AUS) and Miss J.C. Russell (USA) V	Mrs R. Nideffer (RSA) and Miss S. Walsh (USA) 6/1 6/3	Miss R. Casals (USA) and Miss B. F. Stove (NED) 7/6(6) 6/2	Miss J.M. Durie (GBR) and Miss A.E. Smith (USA) 0/6 1/6	2	1	Miss J.M. Durie (GBR) and Miss A.E. Smith (USA) 6/2 6/1
Mrs R. Nideffer (RSA) and Miss S. Walsh (USA) V	Miss H. Mandlikova (AUS) and Miss J.C. Russell (USA) 1/6 3/6	Miss J.M. Durie (GBR) and Miss A.E. Smith (USA) 1/6 3/6	Miss R. Casals (USA) and Miss B. F. Stove (NED) w/o	0	3	
GROUP B						
Miss M. Jausovec (SLO) and Miss Y. Vermaak (RSA) V	Miss W.M. Turnbull (AUS) and Miss S.V. Wade (GBR) 3/6 4/6	Miss L. Charles (GBR) and Miss A. Hobbs (GBR) 5/7 3/6	Miss H. Gourlay (AUS) and Mrs G.E. Reid (AUS) 7/5 6/2	1	2	Miss W.M. Turnbull (AUS) and Miss S.V. Wade (GBR)
Miss W.M. Turnbull (AUS) and Miss S.V. Wade (GBR) V	Miss M. Jausovec (SLO) and Miss Y. Vermaak (RSA) 6/3 6/4	Miss H. Gourlay (AUS) and Mrs G.E. Reid (AUS) 6/2 6/2	Miss L. Charles (GBR) and Miss A. Hobbs (GBR) 6/2 6/3	3	0	
Miss H. Gourlay (AUS) and Mrs G.E. Reid (AUS) V	Miss L. Charles (GBR) and Miss A. Hobbs (GBR) 4/6 4/6	Miss W.M. Turnbull (AUS) and Miss S.V. Wade (GBR) 2/6 2/6	Miss M. Jausovec (SLO) and Miss Y. Vermaak (RSA) 5/7 2/6	0	3	
Miss L. Charles (GBR) and Miss A. Hobbs (GBR) V	Miss H. Gourlay (AUS) and Mrs G.E. Reid (AUS) 6/4 6/4	Miss M. Jausovec (SLO) and Miss Y. Vermaak (RSA) 7/5 6/3	Miss W.M. Turnbull (AUS) and Miss S.V. Wade (GBR) 2/6 3/6	2	1	

This event is played on a 'round robin' basis. Eight invited pairs are divided into two groups and each pair in each group plays the others. The pairs winning most matches are the winners of their respective groups and play a final round as indicated above. If matches should be equal in any group, the head-to-head result between the two pairs with the same number of wins determines the winning pair of the group.

Heavy type denotes seeded players.
The matches are the best of three sets

ALPHABETICAL LIST – 35 & OVER EVENTS

GENTLEMEN

Amritraj A. (India)
Amritraj V. (India)
Bahrami M. (Iran)
Bates M.J. (Great Britain)
Curren K. (USA)
Donnelly G. (USA)
Dowdeswell C. (Great Britain)
Dupre P. (USA)

Edmondson M.R. (Australia)
Fibak W.J. (Poland)
Fitzgerald J.B. (Australia)
Frawley R.J. (Australia)
Gilbert B. (USA)
Guenthardt H. (Switzerland)
Jarrett A.M. (Great Britain)
Jarryd A. (Sweden)

Kriek J.C. (USA)
Krishnan R. (India)
Mayer A.A. (USA)
Mayer G. (USA)
Mayotte T. (USA)
McNamara P.B. (Australia)
McNamee P.F. (Australia)
Mottram C.J. (Great Britain)

Pfister H. (USA)
Shiras L. (USA)
Slozil P. (Czech Republic)
Smid T. (Czech Republic)
Smith J.R. (Great Britain)
Taroczy B. (Hungary)
Visser D. (South Africa)
Wilkison T. (USA)

LADIES

Casals Miss R. (USA)
Charles Miss L. (Great Britain)
Durie Miss J.M. (Great Britain)
Gourlay Miss H. (Australia)

Hobbs Miss A. (Great Britain)
Jausovec Miss M. (Slovenia)
Mandlikova Miss H. (Australia)
Nideffer Mrs R. (South Africa)

Reid Mrs G.E. (Australia)
Russell Miss J.C. (USA)
Smith Miss A.E. (USA)
Stove Miss B.F. (Netherlands)

Turnbull Miss W.M. (Australia)
Vermaak Miss Y. (South Africa)
Wade Miss S.V. (Great Britain)
Walsh Miss S. (USA)

ALPHABETICAL LIST – 45 & OVER EVENT

GENTLEMEN

Alexander J.G. (Australia)
Case R.L. (Australia)
Cox M. (Great Britain)
Davidson O.K. (Australia)
Dent P.C. (Australia)
Drysdale E.C. (South Africa)
Feaver J.W. (Great Britain)
Fillol J. (Chile)

Fraser N.A. (Australia)
Gorman T.W. (USA)
Gottfried B.E. (USA)
Gullikson T.R. (USA)
Hewitt R.A.J. (South Africa)
Kodes J. (Czech Republic)
Lutz R.C. (USA)
Masters G. (Australia)

McMillan F.D. (South Africa)
Metreveli A. (Russia)
Nastase I. (Romania)
Newcombe J.D. (Australia)
Okker T.S. (Netherlands)
Riessen M.C. (USA)
Roche A.D. (Australia)
Rosewall K.R. (Australia)

Santana M. (Spain)
Smith S.R. (USA)
Stewart S.E. (USA)
Stockton R.L. (USA)
Stolle F.S. (Australia)
Stone A.J. (Australia)
Tanner R. (USA)
Taylor R. (Great Britain)

Holder: V. Voltchkov

For both the Boys' Singles *and* the Boys' Doubles Championships, the winners become the holders, for the year only, of a Cup presented by The All England Lawn Tennis and Croquet Club. The winners each receive a miniature Cup and the runners-up receive mementoes.

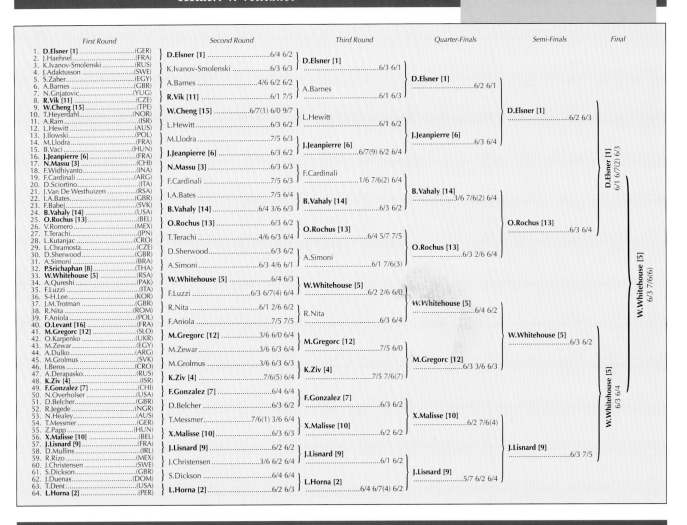

First Round	Second Round	Third Round	Quarter-Finals	Semi-Finals	Final
1. **D.Elsner [1]** ....(GER)	D.Elsner [1] 6/4 6/2	D.Elsner [1]			
2. J.Haehnel ....(FRA)		................................6/3 6/1			
3. K.Ivanov-Smolenski ....(RUS)	K.Ivanov-Smolenski 6/3 6/3		D.Elsner [1]		
4. J.Adaktusson ....(SWE)			........................6/2 6/1		
5. S.Zaher ....(EGY)	A.Barnes 4/6 6/2 6/2	A.Barnes			
6. A.Barnes ....(GBR)		................................6/1 6/3			
7. N.Gnjatovic ....(YUG)	R.Vik [11] 6/1 7/5			D.Elsner [1]	
8. **R.Vik [11]** ....(CZE)				....................6/2 6/3	
9. **W.Cheng [15]** ....(TPE)	W.Cheng [15] ....6/7(1) 6/0 9/7	L.Hewitt			
10. T.Heyerdahl ....(NOR)		................................6/1 6/2			
11. A.Ram ....(ISR)	L.Hewitt 7/5 6/3		J.Jeanpierre [6]		
12. L.Hewitt ....(AUS)			........................6/3 6/4		
13. J.Ilowski ....(POL)	M.Llodra 7/5 6/3	J.Jeanpierre [6]			
14. M.Llodra ....(FRA)		......................6/7(9) 6/2 6/4			
15. B.Vaci ....(HUN)	J.Jeanpierre [6] 6/3 6/2				D.Elsner [1]
16. **J.Jeanpierre [6]** ....(FRA)					.............6/1 6/7(2) 6/3
17. **N.Massu [3]** ....(CHI)	N.Massu [3] 6/3 6/3	F.Cardinali			
18. F.Widhiyanto ....(INA)		............................1/6 7/6(2) 6/4			
19. F.Cardinali ....(ARG)	F.Cardinali 7/5 6/3		B.Vahaly [14]		
20. D.Sciortino ....(ITA)			..................3/6 7/6(2) 6/4		
21. J.Van De Westhuizen ....(RSA)	I.A.Bates 7/5 6/4	B.Vahaly [14]			
22. **I.A.Bates** ....(GBR)		................................6/3 6/2			
23. F.Babej ....(SVK)	B.Vahaly [14] 6/4 3/6 6/3			O.Rochus [13]	
24. **B.Vahaly [14]** ....(USA)				....................6/3 6/4	
25. **O.Rochus [13]** ....(BEL)	O.Rochus [13] 6/3 6/2	O.Rochus [13]			
26. V.Romero ....(MEX)		............................6/4 5/7 7/5			
27. T.Terachi ....(JPN)	T.Terachi 4/6 6/3 6/4		O.Rochus [13]		
28. L.Kutanjac ....(CRO)			........................6/3 2/6 6/4		
29. L.Chramosta ....(CZE)	D.Sherwood 6/3 6/2	A.Simoni			
30. D.Sherwood ....(GBR)		............................6/1 7/6(3)			
31. A.Simoni ....(BRA)	A.Simoni 6/3 4/6 6/1				
32. **P.Srichaphan [8]** ....(THA)					W.Whitehouse [5]
33. **W.Whitehouse [5]** ....(RSA)	W.Whitehouse [5] 6/4 6/3	W.Whitehouse [5]			6/3 7/6(6)
34. A.Qureshi ....(PAK)		..........................6/2 2/6 6/0			
35. F.Luzzi ....(ITA)	F.Luzzi ....6/3 6/7(4) 6/4		W.Whitehouse [5]		
36. S-H.Lee ....(KOR)			........................6/4 6/2		
37. J.M.Trotman ....(GBR)	R.Nita 6/1 2/6 6/2	R.Nita			
38. R.Nita ....(ROM)		................................6/3 6/4			
39. F.Aniola ....(POL)	F.Aniola 7/5 7/5			W.Whitehouse [5]	
40. **O.Levant [16]** ....(FRA)				....................6/3 6/2	
41. **M.Gregorc [12]** ....(SLO)	M.Gregorc [12] 3/6 6/0 6/4	M.Gregorc [12]			
42. O.Karpenko ....(UKR)		................................7/5 6/0			
43. M.Zewar ....(EGY)	M.Zewar 3/6 6/3 6/4		M.Gregorc [12]		
44. A.Dulko ....(ARG)			........................6/3 3/6 6/3		
45. M.Grolmus ....(SVK)	M.Grolmus 3/6 6/3 6/3	K.Ziv [4]			
46. I.Beros ....(CRO)		............................7/5 7/6(7)			
47. A.Derapasko ....(RUS)	K.Ziv [4] ....7/6(5) 6/4				W.Whitehouse [5]
48. **K.Ziv [4]** ....(ISR)					6/3 6/4
49. **F.Gonzalez [7]** ....(CHI)	F.Gonzalez [7] 6/4 6/4	F.Gonzalez [7]			
50. N.Overholser ....(USA)		................................6/3 6/4			
51. D.Belcher ....(GBR)	D.Belcher 6/3 6/2		X.Malisse [10]		
52. R.Jegede ....(NGR)			........................6/2 7/6(4)		
53. N.Healey ....(AUS)	T.Messmer ....7/6(1) 3/6 6/4	X.Malisse [10]			
54. T.Messmer ....(GER)		................................6/2 6/2			
55. Z.Papp ....(HUN)	X.Malisse [10] 6/3 6/3			J.Lisnard [9]	
56. **X.Malisse [10]** ....(BEL)				....................6/3 7/5	
57. **J.Lisnard [9]** ....(FRA)	J.Lisnard [9] 6/2 6/2	J.Lisnard [9]			
58. D.Mullins ....(IRL)		................................6/1 6/2			
59. R.Rizo ....(MEX)	J.Christensen 3/6 6/2 6/4		J.Lisnard [9]		
60. J.Christensen ....(SWE)			..................5/7 6/2 6/4		
61. S.Dickson ....(GBR)	S.Dickson 6/4 6/4	L.Horna [2]			
62. J.Duenas ....(DOM)		......................6/4 6/7(4) 6/2			
63. T.Dent ....(USA)	L.Horna [2] 6/2 6/3				
64. **L.Horna [2]** ....(PER)					

Holders: D. Bracciali and J. Robichaud

There are only 16 pairs in this event

First Round	Second Round	Quarter-Finals	Semi-Finals	Final
1. **L.Horna** (PER) & **N.Massu** (CHI) ....[1]	L.Horna & N.Massu [1]			
2. S-H.Lee (KOR) & T.Terachi (JPN)		..................7/6(4) 6/2	L.Horna & N.Massu [1]	
3. N.Healey (AUS) & L.Hewitt (AUS)	N.Healey & L.Hewitt		..................7/6(4) 6/4	
4. D.Elsner (GER) & T.Messmer (GER)		..................6/4 7/5		L.Horna & N.Massu [1]
5. **J.Haehnel** (FRA) & **J.Jeanpierre** (FRA) ....[3]	A.Dulko & A.Simoni (BRA)			6/3 6/4
6. A.Dulko (ARG) & A.Simoni (BRA)		..................6/4 6/2	F.Luzzi (ITA) & A.Ram (ISR)	
7. P.Srichaphan (THA) & K.Ziv (ISR)	F.Luzzi (ITA) & A.Ram (ISR)		..............7/6(8) 2/6 8/6	
8. F.Luzzi (ITA) & A.Ram (ISR)		..........5/7 7/5 11/9		
9. I.A.Bates (GBR) & M.Gregorc (SLO)	I.A.Bates (GBR) & M.Gregorc (SLO)			L.Horna & N.Massu [1]
10. X.Malisse (BEL) & O.Rochus (BEL)		..................0/0 Ret'd	A.Barnes & K.Ivanov-Smolenski	6/4 6/2
11. A.Barnes (GBR) & K.Ivanov-Smolenski (RUS)	A.Barnes & K.Ivanov-Smolenski		..................6/3 7/5	
12. **D.Sherwood** (GBR) & **J.M.Trotman** (GBR) ....[4]		..................6/2 7/5		
13. S.Dickson (GBR) & D.Kiernan (GBR)	S.Dickson & D.Kiernan			J.Van De Westhuizen & W.Whitehouse [2]
14. F.Cardinali (ARG) & F.Gonzalez (CHI)		..................6/1 6/4	J.Van De Westhuizen & W.Whitehouse [2]	7/6(3) 7/5
15. F.Babej (SVK) & M.Grolmus (SVK)	J.Van De Westhuizen & W.Whitehouse [2]		..............3/6 7/6(5) 6/3	
16. **J.Van De Westhuizen** (RSA) & **W.Whitehouse** (RSA) ....[2]		..................6/4 6/4		

Heavy type denotes seeded players. The figure in brackets against names denotes the order in which they have been seeded.
The matches are the best of three sets

For both the Girls' Singles *and* the Girls' Doubles Championships, the winners become the holders, for the year only, of a Cup presented by The All England Lawn Tennis and Croquet Club. The winners each receive a miniature Cup and the runners-up receive mementoes.

Holder: Miss A. Mauresmo

First Round	Second Round	Third Round	Quarter-Finals	Semi-Finals	Final
1. Miss L.Wood (GBR)	Miss N.Grandin 6/1 6/4	Miss R.Fujiwara .... 7/6(7) 6/2	Miss H.Collin 6/1 6/4	Miss A.Rippner [6] 6/1 6/4	Miss A.Rippner [6] 6/1 6/2
2. Miss N.Grandin (RSA)					
3. Miss R.Fujiwara (JPN)	Miss R.Fujiwara 6/3 6/4				
4. Miss G.Volekova (SVK)					
5. Miss S.Taylor (USA)	Miss H.Collin 6/2 6/2	Miss H.Collin 6/2 6/4			
6. Miss H.Collin (GBR)					
7. Miss H.Danilidou (GRE)	Miss K.Srebotnik [12] 7/5 6/3				
8. **Miss K.Srebotnik [12]** (SLO)					
9. **Miss Y-J.Cho [9]** (KOR)	Miss Y-J.Cho [9] 3/6 6/1 6/2	Miss M.Irvin 6/4 6/2	Miss A.Rippner [6] 6/2 6/1		
10. Miss L.Sanchez (FRA)					
11. Miss P.Arrangoiz (MEX)	Miss M.Irvin 6/4 6/3				
12. Miss M.Irvin (USA)					
13. Miss D.Krstulovic (CRO)	Miss K.Elliott 7/5 6/3	Miss A.Rippner [6] 6/4 6/4			
14. Miss K.Elliott (GBR)					
15. Miss O.Rejniak (POL)	Miss A.Rippner [6] 6/1 6/3				
16. **Miss A.Rippner [6]** (USA)					
17. **Miss E.Dominjkovic [4]** (AUS)	Miss E.Dominjkovic [4] 6/2 6/4	Miss M.Iversen 7/5 6/4	Miss A.Morigami [11] 6/4 6/2	Miss A.Morigami [11] 6/3 6/3	
18. Miss R.Teperberg (ISR)					
19. Miss C.Coombs (GBR)	Miss M.Iversen 6/0 6/4				
20. Miss M.Iversen (DEN)					
21. Miss M.Sequera (VEN)	Miss M.Sequera .... 6/3 7/6(6)	Miss A.Morigami [11] 6/4 6/3			
22. Miss J.Osman (GBR)					
23. Miss W.Prakusya (INA)	Miss A.Morigami [11] .... 6/2 7/6(3)				
24. **Miss A.Morigami [11]** (JPN)					
25. **Miss C.Popescu [15]** (CAN)	Miss C.Popescu [15] .... 6/7(3) 7/6(6) 6/3	Miss Z.Gubacsi 2/6 7/5 6/1	Miss Z.Gubacsi 6/1 6/1		
26. Miss S.Urickova (SVK)					
27. Miss I.Bracun (CRO)	Miss Z.Gubacsi 6/1 6/2				
28. Miss Z.Gubacsi (HUN)					
29. Miss S.Lydon (GBR)	Miss L.Van Rooyen .... 7/6(3) 6/0	Miss J.Woehr [5] 7/5 6/4			
30. Miss L.Van Rooyen (RSA)					
31. Miss C.Castano (COL)	Miss J.Woehr [5] 6/4 6/1				
32. **Miss J.Woehr [5]** (GER)					
33. **Miss E.Syssoeva [8]** (RUS)	Miss M.Matevzic 7/5	Miss S.Rizzi 2/6 6/3 6/2	Miss I.Selyutina [14] .... 7/6(15) 6/1	Miss C.Black [3] 6/0 6/2	Miss C.Black [3] 6/3 7/5
34. Miss M.Matevzic (SLO)					
35. Miss L.Herbert (GBR)	Miss S.Rizzi 6/2				
36. Miss S.Rizzi (FRA)					
37. Miss I.Visic (CRO)	Miss I.Visic 6/5	Miss I.Selyutina [14] 6/2 6/2			
38. Miss J.White (GBR)					
39. Miss B.Braverman (USA)	Miss I.Selyutina [14] 6/2 6/2				
40. **Miss I.Selyutina [14]** (KAZ)					
41. **Miss A.Sebova [16]** (SVK)	Miss A.Sebova [16] 7/5 6/1	Miss A.Grahame .... 6/0 7/6(5)	Miss C.Black [3] 6/4 6/4		
42. Miss S.Turner (GBR)					
43. Miss A.Grahame (AUS)	Miss A.Grahame .... 7/6(5)				
44. Miss B.Mouhtassine (MAR)					
45. Miss E.Dyrberg (DEN)	Miss E.Dyrberg 6/3 6/3	Miss C.Black [3] 6/3 6/4			
46. Miss A.Pillay (RSA)					
47. Miss M.Niroj (THA)	Miss C.Black [3] 6/2 6/2				
48. **Miss C.Black [3]** (ZIM)					
49. **Miss T.Poutchek [7]** (BLR)	Miss T.Poutchek [7] 6/1 6/1	Miss A.Tordoff 2/6 6/4 9/7	Miss B.Stewart [13] 6/3 6/3	Miss B.Stewart [13] 6/3 5/7 7/5	
50. Miss S.Bajin (CAN)					
51. Miss K.Chevalier (FRA)	Miss A.Tordoff 2/6 6/0 6/3				
52. Miss A.Tordoff (GBR)					
53. Miss L.Dell'angelo (ITA)	Miss P.Palencia .... 5/7 7/6(1) 6/1	Miss B.Stewart [13] 6/0 3/6 6/4			
54. Miss P.Palencia (MEX)					
55. Miss J.T.Singian (USA)	Miss B.Stewart [13] 7/5 6/4				
56. **Miss B.Stewart [13]** (AUS)					
57. **Miss M.Inoue [10]** (JPN)	Miss B.Colosio .... 7/6(5) 4/6 6/4	Miss H.Farr 4/6 6/3 8/6	Miss J.Henin 6/0 6/2		
58. Miss B.Colosio (BRA)					
59. Miss G.Lastra (USA)	Miss H.Farr 4/6 7/5 6/3				
60. Miss H.Farr (GBR)					
61. Miss T.Callow (GBR)	Miss J.Henin 6/2 6/2	Miss J.Henin 7/5 6/4			
62. Miss J.Henin (BEL)					
63. Miss N.J.Woodhouse (GBR)	Miss R.Sandu [2] 1/6 2/6				
64. **Miss R.Sandu [2]** (ROM)					

THE GIRLS' DOUBLES CHAMPIONSHIP

Holders: Miss O. Barabanschikova and Miss A. Mauresmo

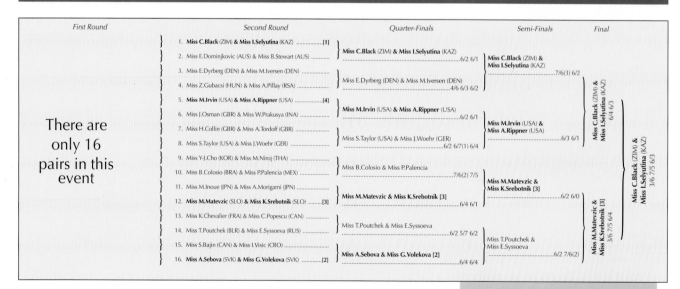

There are only 16 pairs in this event

First Round	Second Round	Quarter-Finals	Semi-Finals	Final
1. **Miss C.Black (ZIM) & Miss I.Selyutina (KAZ)** [1]	Miss C.Black (ZIM) & Miss I.Selyutina (KAZ) 6/2 6/1	Miss C.Black (ZIM) & Miss I.Selyutina (KAZ) .... 7/6(3) 6/2	Miss C.Black (ZIM) & Miss I.Selyutina (KAZ) 6/4 6/3	Miss C.Black (ZIM) & Miss I.Selyutina (KAZ) 3/6 7/5 6/3
2. Miss E.Dominjkovic (AUS) & Miss B.Stewart (AUS)				
3. Miss E.Dyrberg (DEN) & Miss M.Iversen (DEN)	Miss E.Dyrberg (DEN) & Miss M.Iversen (DEN) 4/6 6/3 6/2			
4. Miss Z.Gubacsi (HUN) & Miss A.Pillay (RSA)				
5. **Miss M.Irvin (USA) & Miss A.Rippner (USA)** [4]	Miss M.Irvin (USA) & Miss A.Rippner (USA) 6/2 6/1	Miss M.Irvin (USA) & Miss A.Rippner (USA) .... 6/2 6/7(1) 6/4	Miss M.Irvin (USA) & Miss A.Rippner (USA) 6/3 6/1	
6. Miss J.Osman (GBR) & Miss W.Prakusya (INA)				
7. Miss H.Collin (GBR) & Miss A.Tordoff (GBR)	Miss S.Taylor (USA) & Miss J.Woehr (GER)			
8. Miss S.Taylor (USA) & Miss J.Woehr (GER)				
9. Miss Y-J.Cho (KOR) & Miss M.Niroj (THA)	Miss B.Colosio & Miss P.Palencia .... 7/6(2) 7/5	Miss M.Matevzic & Miss K.Srebotnik [3] 6/2 6/0	Miss M.Matevzic & Miss K.Srebotnik [3] 3/6 7/5 6/4	
10. Miss B.Colosio (BRA) & Miss P.Palencia (MEX)				
11. Miss M.Inoue (JPN) & Miss A.Morigami (JPN)	Miss M.Matevzic & Miss K.Srebotnik [3] 6/4 6/1			
12. **Miss M.Matevzic (SLO) & Miss K.Srebotnik (SLO)** [3]				
13. Miss K.Chevalier (FRA) & Miss C.Popescu (CAN)	Miss T.Poutchek & Miss E.Syssoeva 6/2 5/7 6/2	Miss T.Poutchek & Miss E.Syssoeva .... 6/2 7/6(2)		
14. Miss T.Poutchek (BLR) & Miss E.Syssoeva (RUS)				
15. Miss S.Bajin (CAN) & Miss I.Visic (CRO)	Miss A.Sebova & Miss G.Volekova [2] 6/4 6/4			
16. **Miss A.Sebova (SVK) & Miss G.Volekova (SVK)** [2]				

Heavy type denotes seeded players. The figure in brackets against names denotes the order in which they have been seeded.

The matches are the best of three sets

Champions and Runners-up

1877 - S. W. Gore
W. C. Marshall

1878 - P. F. Hadow
S. W. Gore

★ 1879 - J. T. Hartley
V. St. L. Goold

1880 - J. T. Hartley
H. F. Lawford

1881 - W. Renshaw
J. T. Hartley

1882 - W. Renshaw
E. Renshaw

1883 - W. Renshaw
E. Renshaw

1884 - W. Renshaw
H. F. Lawford

1885 - W. Renshaw
H. F. Lawford

1886 - W. Renshaw
H. F. Lawford

★ 1887 - H. F. Lawford
E. Renshaw

1888 - E. Renshaw
H. F. Lawford

1889 - W. Renshaw
E. Renshaw

1890 - W. J. Hamilton
W. Renshaw

★ 1891 - W. Baddeley
J. Pim

1892 - W. Baddeley
J. Pim

1893 - J. Pim
W. Baddeley

1894 - J. Pim
W. Baddeley

★ 1895 - W. Baddeley
W. V. Eaves

1896 - H. S. Mahony
W. Baddeley

1897 - R. F. Doherty
H. S. Mahony

1898 - R. F. Doherty
H. L. Doherty

1899 - R. F. Doherty
A. W. Gore

1900 - R. F. Doherty
S. H. Smith

1901 - A. W. Gore
R. F. Doherty

1902 - H. L. Doherty
A. W. Gore

1903 - H. L. Doherty
F. L. Riseley

1904 - H. L. Doherty
F. L. Riseley

1905 - H. L. Doherty
N. E. Brookes

1906 - H. L. Doherty
F. L. Riseley

★ 1907 - N. E. Brookes
A. W. Gore

★ 1908 - A. W. Gore
H. Roper Barrett

1909 - A. W. Gore
M. J. G. Ritchie

1910 - A. F. Wilding
A. W. Gore

1911 - A. F. Wilding
H. Roper Barrett

1912 - A. F. Wilding
A. W. Gore

1913 - A. F. Wilding
M. E. McLoughlin

1914 - N. E. Brookes
A. F. Wilding

1919 - G. L. Patterson
N. E. Brookes

1920 - W. T. Tilden
G. L. Patterson

1921 - W. T. Tilden
B. I. C. Norton

★†1922 - G. L. Patterson
R. Lycett

1923 - W. M. Johnston
F. T. Hunter

1924 - J. Borotra
R. Lacoste

1925 - R. Lacoste
J. Borotra

1926 - J. Borotra
H. Kinsey

1927 - H. Cochet
J. Borotra

1928 - R. Lacoste
H. Cochet

1929 - H. Cochet
J. Borotra

1930 - W. T. Tilden
W. Allison

1931 - S. B. Wood
F. X. Shields

1932 - H. E. Vines
H. W. Austin

1933 - J. H. Crawford
H. E. Vines

1934 - F. J. Perry
J. H. Crawford

1935 - F. J. Perry
G. von Cramm

1936 - F. J. Perry
G. von Cramm

★ 1937 - J. D. Budge
G. von Cramm

1938 - J. D. Budge
H. W. Austin

★ 1939 - R. L. Riggs
E. T. Cooke

★ 1946 - Y. Petra
G. E. Brown

1947 - J. Kramer
T. Brown

★ 1948 - R. Falkenburg
J. E. Bromwich

1949 - F. R. Schroeder
J. Drobny

★ 1950 - B. Patty
F. A. Sedgman

1951 - R. Savitt
K. McGregor

1952 - F. A. Sedgman
J. Drobny

★ 1953 - V. Seixas
K. Nielsen

1954 - J. Drobny
K. R. Rosewall

1955 - T. Trabert
K. Nielsen

★ 1956 - L. A. Hoad
K. R. Rosewall

1957 - L. A. Hoad
A. J. Cooper

★ 1958 - A. J. Cooper
N. A. Fraser

★ 1959 - A. Olmedo
R. Laver

★ 1960 - N. A. Fraser
R. Laver

1961 - R. Laver
C. R. McKinley

1962 - R. Laver
M. F. Mulligan

★ 1963 - C. R. McKinley
F. S. Stolle

1964 - R. Emerson
F. S. Stolle

1965 - R. Emerson
F. S. Stolle

1966 - M. Santana
R. D. Ralston

1967 - J. D. Newcombe
W. P. Bungert

1968 - R. Laver
A. D. Roche

1969 - R. Laver
J. D. Newcombe

1970 - J. D. Newcombe
K. R. Rosewall

1971 - J. D. Newcombe
S. R. Smith

★ 1972 - S. R. Smith
I. Nastase

★ 1973 - J. Kodes
A. Metreveli

1974 - J. S. Connors
K. R. Rosewall

1975 - A. R. Ashe
J. S. Connors

1976 - B. Borg
I. Nastase

1977 - B. Borg
J. S. Connors

1978 - B. Borg
J. S. Connors

1979 - B. Borg
R. Tanner

1980 - B. Borg
J. P. McEnroe

1981 - J. P. McEnroe
B. Borg

1982 - J. S. Connors
J. P. McEnroe

1983 - J. P. McEnroe
C. J. Lewis

1984 - J. P. McEnroe
J. S. Connors

1985 - B. Becker
K. Curren

1986 - B.Becker
I. Lendl

1987 - P. Cash
I. Lendl

1988 - S. Edberg
B. Becker

1989 - B. Becker
S. Edberg

1990 - S. Edberg
B. Becker

1991 - M. Stich
B. Becker

1992 - A. Agassi
G. Ivanisevic

1993 - P. Sampras
J. Courier

1994 - P. Sampras
G. Ivanisevic

1995 - P. Sampras
B. Becker

1996 - R. Krajicek
M. Washington

NOTE: For the years 1913, 1914 and 1919-23 inclusive the Championship Roll includes the 'World's Championship on Grass' granted to The Lawn Tennis Association by The International Lawn Tennis Federation. This title was then abolished and commencing in 1924 they became The Official Lawn Tennis Championships recognised by The International Lawn Tennis Federation. Prior to 1922 the holders in the singles events and the gentlemen's doubles did not compete in The Championships but met the winners of these events in the Challenge Rounds.
† Challenge Round abolished; holders subsequently played through.   *The holder did not defend the title.

Champions and Runners-up

1884 - Miss M. Watson
 Miss L. Watson

1885 - Miss M. Watson
 Miss B. Bingley

1886 - Miss B. Bingley
 Miss M. Watson

1887 - Miss L. Dod
 Miss B. Bingley

1888 - Miss L. Dod
 Mrs. G. W. Hillyard

★1889 - Mrs. G. W. Hillyard
 Miss L. Rice

★1890 - Miss L. Rice
 Miss M. Jacks

★1891 - Miss L. Dod
 Mrs. G. W. Hillyard

1892 - Miss L. Dod
 Mrs. G. W. Hillyard

1893 - Miss L. Dod
 Mrs. G. W. Hillyard

★1894 - Mrs. G. W. Hillyard
 Miss E. L. Austin

★1895 - Miss C. Cooper
 Miss H. Jackson

1896 - Miss C. Cooper
 Mrs. W. H.Pickering

1897 - Mrs. G. W. Hillyard
 Miss C. Cooper

★1898 - Miss C. Cooper
 Miss L Martin

1899 - Mrs. G. W. Hillyard
 Miss C. Cooper

1900 - Mrs. G. W. Hillyard
 Miss C. Cooper

1901 - Mrs. A. Sterry
 Mrs. G. W. Hillyard

1902 - Miss M. E. Robb
 Mrs. A. Sterry

★1903 - Miss D. K. Douglass
 Miss E. W. Thomson

1904 - Miss D. K. Douglass
 Mrs. A. Sterry

1905 - Miss M. Sutton
 Miss D. K. Douglass

1906 - Miss D. K Douglass
 Miss M. Sutton

1907 - Miss M. Sutton
 Mrs. Lambert Chambers

★1908 - Mrs. A. Sterry
 Miss A. M. Morton

★1909 - Miss D. P. Boothby
 Miss A. M. Morton

1910 - Mrs. Lambert Chambers
 Miss D. P. Boothby

1911 - Mrs. Lambert Chambers
 Miss D. P. Boothby

★1912 - Mrs. D. R. Larcombe
 Mrs. A. Sterry

★1913 - Mrs. Lambert Chambers
 Mrs. R. J. McNair

1914 - Mrs. Lambert Chambers
 Mrs. D. R. Larcombe

1919 - Mlle. S. Lenglen
 Mrs. Lambert Chambers

1920 - Mlle. S. Lenglen
 Mrs. Lambert Chambers

1921 - Mlle. S. Lenglen
 Miss E. Ryan

†1922 - Mlle. S. Lenglen
 Mrs. F. Mallory

1923 - Mlle. S. Lenglen
 Miss K. McKane

1924 - Miss K. McKane
 Miss H. Wills

1925 - Mlle. S. Lenglen
 Miss J. Fry

1926 - Mrs. L. A. Godfree
 Sta. L. de Alvarez

★1927 - Miss H. Wills
 Sta. L. de Alvarez

1928 - Miss H. Wills
 Sta. L. de Alvarez

1929 - Miss H. Wills
 Miss H. H. Jacobs

1930 - Mrs. F. S. Moody
 Miss E. Ryan

★1931 - Fraulein C. Aussem
 Fraulein H. Krahwinkel

1932 - Mrs. F. S. Moody
 Miss H. H. Jacobs

1933 - Mrs. F. S. Moody
 Miss D. E. Round

★1934 - Miss D. E. Round
 Miss H. H. Jacobs

1935 - Mrs. F. S. Moody
 Miss H. H. Jacobs

★1936 - Miss H. H. Jacobs
 Frau. S. Sperling

1937 - Miss D. E. Round
 Miss J. Jedrzejowska

1938 - Mrs. F. S. Moody
 Miss H. H. Jacobs

★1939 - Miss A. Marble
 Miss K. E. Stammers

★1946 - Miss P. Betz
 Miss L. Brough

★1947 - Miss M. Osborne
 Miss D. Hart

1948 - Miss L. Brough
 Miss D. Hart

1949 - Miss L. Brough
 Mrs. W. du Pont

1950 - Miss L. Brough
 Mrs. W. du Pont

1951 - Miss D. Hart
 Miss S. Fry

1952 - Miss M. Connolly
 Miss L. Brough

1953 - Miss M. Connolly
 Miss D. Hart

1954 - Miss M. Connolly
 Miss L. Brough

★1955 - Miss L. Brough
 Mrs. J. G. Fleitz

1956 - Miss S. Fry
 Miss A. Buxton

★1957 - Miss A. Gibson
 Miss D. R. Hard

1958 - Miss A. Gibson
 Miss A. Mortimer

★1959 - Miss M. E. Bueno
 Miss D. R. Hard

1960 - Miss M. E. Bueno
 Miss S. Reynolds

★1961 - Miss A. Mortimer
 Miss C. C. Truman

1962 - Mrs. J. R. Susman
 Mrs. V. Sukova

★1963 - Miss M. Smith
 Miss B. J. Moffitt

1964 - Miss M. E. Bueno
 Miss M. Smith

1965 - Miss M. Smith
 Miss M. E. Bueno

1966 - Mrs. L. W. King
 Miss M. E. Bueno

1967 - Mrs. L. W. King
 Mrs. P. F. Jones

1968 - Mrs. L. W. King
 Miss J. A. M. Tegart

1969 - Mrs. P. F. Jones
 Mrs. L. W. King

★1970 - Mrs. B. M. Court
 Mrs. L. W. King

1971 - Miss E. F. Goolagong
 Mrs. B. M. Court

1972 - Mrs. L. W. King
 Miss E. F. Goolagong

1973 - Mrs. L. W. King
 Miss C. M. Evert

1974 - Miss C. M. Evert
 Mrs. O. Morozova

1975 - Mrs. L. W. King
 Mrs. R. Cawley

★1976 - Miss C. M. Evert
 Mrs. R. Cawley

1977 - Miss S. V. Wade
 Miss B. F. Stove

1978 - Miss M. Navratilova
 Miss C. M. Evert

1979 - Miss M. Navratilova
 Mrs. J. M. Lloyd

1980 - Mrs. R. Cawley
 Mrs. J. M. Lloyd

1981 - Mrs. J. M. Lloyd
 Miss H. Mandlikova

1982 - Miss M. Navratilova
 Mrs. J. M. Lloyd

1983 - Miss M. Navratilova
 Miss A. Jaeger

1984 - Miss M. Navratilova
 Mrs. J. M. Lloyd

1985 - Miss M. Navratilova
 Mrs. J. M. Lloyd

1986 - Miss M. Navratilova
 Miss H. Mandlikova

1987 - Miss M. Navratilova
 Miss S. Graf

1988 - Miss S. Graf
 Miss M. Navratilova

1989 - Miss S. Graf
 Miss M. Navratilova

1990 - Miss M. Navratilova
 Miss Z. Garrison

1991 - Miss S. Graf
 Miss G. Sabatini

1992 - Miss S. Graf
 Miss M. Seles

1993 - Miss S. Graf
 Miss J. Novotna

1994 - Miss C. Martinez
 Miss M. Navratilova

1995 - Miss S. Graf
 Miss A. Sanchez Vicario

1996 - Miss S. Graf
 Miss A. Sanchez Vicario

MAIDEN NAMES OF LADY CHAMPIONS

In the tables the following have been recorded in both married and single identities.

Mrs. R. Cawley ....Miss E. F. Goolagong		Mrs. F. S. Moody ....Miss H. Wills
Mrs. Lambert Chambers ....Miss D. K. Douglass		Mrs. O. Morozova ....Miss O. Morozova
Mrs. B. M. Court ....Miss M. Smith	Mrs. G. W. Hillyard ....Miss B. Bingley	Mrs. L. E. G. Price ....Miss S. Reynolds
Mrs. B. C. Covell ....Miss P. L. Howkins	Mrs. P. F. Jones ....Miss A. S. Haydon	Mrs. G. E. Reid ....Miss K. Melville
Mrs. D. E. Dalton ....Miss J. A. M. Tegart	Mrs. L. W. King ....Miss B. J. Moffitt	Mrs. P. D. Smylie ....Miss E. M. Sayers
Mrs. W. du Pont ....Miss M. Osborne	Mrs. M. R. King ....Miss P. E. Mudford	Frau. S. Sperling ....Fraulein H. Krahwinkel
Mrs. L. A. Godfree ....Miss K. McKane	Mrs. D. R. Larcombe ....Miss E. W. Thomson	Mrs. A. Sterry ....Miss C. Cooper
Mrs. H. F. Gourlay Cawley ....Miss H. F. Gourlay	Mrs. J. M. Lloyd ....Miss C. M. Evert	Mrs. J. R. Susman ....Miss K. Hantze

GENTLEMEN'S DOUBLES

1879 - L. R. Erskine and H. F. Lawford
F. Durant and G. E. Tabor

1880 - W. Renshaw and E. Renshaw
O. E. Woodhouse and C. J. Cole

1881 - W. Renshaw and E. Renshaw
W. J. Down and H. Vaughan

1882 - J. T. Hartley and R. T. Richardson
J. G. Horn and C. B. Russell

1883 - C. W. Grinstead and C. E. Welldon
C. B. Russell and R. T. Milford

1884 - W. Renshaw and E. Renshaw
E. W. Lewis and E.L Williams

1885 - W. Renshaw and E. Renshaw
C. E. Farrer and A. J. Stanley

1886 - W. Renshaw and E. Renshaw
C. E. Farrer and A. J. Stanley

1887 - P. Bowes-Lyon and H. W. W. Wilberforce
J. H. Crispe and E. Barratt Smith

1888 - W. Renshaw and E. Renshaw
P Bowes-Lyon and H. W. W. Wilberforce

1889 - W. Renshaw and E. Renshaw
E. W. Lewis and G. W. Hillyard

1890 - J. Pim and F. O. Stoker
E. W. Lewis and G. W. Hillyard

1891 - W. Baddeley and H. Baddeley
J. Pim and F. O. Stoker

1892 - H. S. Barlow and E. W. Lewis
W. Baddeley and H. Baddeley

1893 - J. Pim and F. O. Stoker
E. W. Lewis and H. S. Barlow

1894 - W. Baddeley and H. Baddeley
H. S. Barlow and C. H. Martin

1895 - W. Baddeley and H. Baddeley
E. W. Lewis and W. V. Eaves

1896 - W. Baddeley and H. Baddeley
R. F. Doherty and H. A. Nisbet

1897 - R. F. Doherty and H. L. Doherty
W. Baddeley and H. Baddeley

1898 - R. F. Doherty and H. L . Doherty
H. A. Nisbet and C. Hobart

1899 - R. F. Doherty and H. L. Doherty
H. A. Nisbet and C. Hobart

1900 - R. F. Doherty and H. L. Doherty
H. Roper Barrett and H. A. Nisbet

1901 - R. F. Doherty and H. L. Doherty
Dwight Davis and Holcombe Ward

1902 - S. H. Smith and F. L. Riseley
R. F. Doherty and H. L. Doherty

1903 - R. F. Doherty and H. L. Doherty
S. H. Smith and F. L. Riseley

1904 - R. F. Doherty and H. L. Doherty
S. H. Smith and F. L. Riseley

1905 - R. F. Doherty and H. L. Doherty
S. H. Smith and F. L. Riseley

1906 - S. H. Smith and F. L. Riseley
R. F. Doherty and H. L. Doherty

1907 - N. E. Brooks and A. F. Wilding
B. C. Wright and K. H. Behr

1908 - A. F. Wilding and M. J. G. Ritchie
A. W. Gore and H. Roper Barrett

1909 - A. W. Gore and H. Roper Barrett
S. N. Doust and H. A. Parker

1910 - A. F. Wilding and M. J. G. Ritchie
A. W. Gore and H. Roper Barrett

1911 - M. Decugis and A. H. Gobert
M. J. G. Ritchie and A. F. Wilding

1912 - H. Roper Barrett and C. P. Dixon
M. Decugis and A. H. Gobert

1913 - H. Roper Barrett and C. P. Dixon
F. W. Rahe and H. Kleinschroth

1914 - N. E. Brookes and A. F. Wilding
H. Roper Barrett and C. P. Dixon

1919 - R. V. Thomas and P. O'Hara-Wood
R. Lycett and R. W. Heath

1920 - R. N. Williams and C. S. Garland
A. R. F. Kingscote and J. C. Parke

1921 - R. Lycett and M. Woosnam
F. G. Lowe and A. H. Lowe

1922 - R. Lycett and J. O. Anderson
G. L. Patterson and P. O'Hara-Wood

1923 - R. Lycett and L. A. Godfree
Count de Gomar and E. Flaquer

1924 - F. T. Hunter and V. Richards
R. N. Williams and W. M. Washburn

1925 - J. Borotra and R. Lacoste
J. Hennessey and R. Casey

1926 - H. Cochet and J. Brugnon
V. Richards and H. Kinsey

1927 - F. T. Hunter and W. T. Tilden
J. Brugnon and H. Cochet

1928 - H. Cochet and J. Brugnon
G. L. Patterson and J. B. Hawkes

1929 - W. Allison and J. Van Ryn
J. C. Gregory and I. G. Collins

1930 - W. Allison and J. Van Ryn
J. H. Doeg and G. M. Lott

1931 - G. M Lott and J. Van Ryn
H. Cochet and J. Brugnon

1932 - J. Borotra and J. Brugnon
G. P. Hughes and F. J. Perry

1933 - J. Borotra and J. Brugnon
R. Nunoi and J. Satoh

1934 - G. M. Lott and L. R. Stoefen
J. Borotra and J. Brugnon

1935 - J. H. Crawford and A. K . Quist
W. Allison and J. Van Ryn

1936 - G. P. Hughes and C. R. D. Tuckey
C. E. Hare and F. H. D. Wilde

1937 - J. D. Budge and G. Mako
G. P. Hughes and C. R. D. Tuckey

1938 - J. D. Budge and G. Mako
H. Henkel and G. von Metaxa

1939 - R. L. Riggs and E. T. Cooke
C. E. Hare and F. H. D. Wilde

1946 - T. Brown and J. Kramer
G. E. Brown and D. Pails

1947 - R. Falkenburg and J. Kramer
A. J. Mottram and O. W. Sidwell

1948 - J. E. Bromwich and F. A. Sedgman
T. Brown and G. Mulloy

1949 - R. Gonzales and F. Parker
G. Mulloy and F. R. Schroeder

1950 - J. E. Bromwich and A. K. Quist
G. E. Brown and O. W Sidwell

1951 - K. McGregor and F. A. Sedgman
J. Drobny and E. W. Sturgess

1952 - K. McGregor and F. A. Sedgman
V. Seixas and E. W. Sturgess

1953 - L. A. Hoad and K. R. Rosewall
R. N. Hartwig and M. G. Rose

1954 - R. N. Hartwig and M. G. Rose
V. Seixas and T. Trabert

1955 - R. N. Hartwig and L. A. Hoad
N. A. Fraser and K. R. Rosewall

1956 - L. A. Hoad and K. R. Rosewall
N. Pietrangeli and O. Sirola

1957 - G. Mulloy and B. Patty
N. A. Fraser and L. A. Hoad

1958 - S. Davidson and U. Schmidt
A. J. Cooper and N. A. Fraser

1959 - R. Emerson and N. A. Fraser
R. Laver and R. Mark

1960 - R. H. Osuna and R. D. Ralston
M. G. Davies and R. K. Wilson

1961 - R. Emerson and N. A. Fraser
R. A. J. Hewitt and F. S. Stolle

1962 - R. A. J. Hewitt and F. S. Stolle
B. Jovanovic and N. Pilic

1963 - R. H. Osuna and A. Palafox
J. C. Barclay and P. Darmon

1964 - R. A. J. Hewitt and F. S. Stolle
R. Emerson and K. N. Fletcher

1965 - J. D. Newcombe and A. D. Roche
K. N. Fletcher and R. A. J. Hewitt

1966 - K. N. Fletcher and J. D. Newcombe
W. W. Bowrey and O. K. Davidson

1967 - R. A. J. Hewitt and F. D. McMillan
R. Emerson and K. N. Fletcher

1968 - J. D. Newcombe and A. D. Roche
K. R. Rosewall and F. S. Stolle

1969 - J. D. Newcombe and A. D. Roche
T. S. Okker and M. C. Reissen

1970 - J. D. Newcombe and A. D. Roche
K. R. Rosewall and F. S. Stolle

1971 - R. S. Emerson and R. G. Laver
A. R. Ashe and R. D. Ralston

1972 - R. A. J. Hewitt and F. D. McMillan
S. R. Smith and E. J. van Dillen

1973 - J. S. Connors and I. Nastase
J. R. Cooper and N. A. Fraser

1974 - J. D. Newcombe and A. D. Roche
R. C. Lutz and S. R. Smith

1975 - V. Gerulaitis and A. Mayer
C. Dowdeswell and A. J. Stone

1976 - B. E. Gottfried and R. Ramirez
R. L. Case and G. Masters

1977 - R. L. Case and G. Masters
J. G. Alexander and P. C. Dent

1978 - R. A. J. Hewitt and F. D. McMillan
P. Fleming and J. P. McEnroe

1979 - P. Fleming and J. P . McEnroe
B. E. Gottfried and R. Ramirez

1980 - P. McNamara and P. McNamee
R. C. Lutz and S. R. Smith

1981 - P. Fleming and J. P. McEnroe
R. C. Lutz and S. R. Smith

1982 - P. McNamara and P. McNamee
P. Fleming and J. P. McEnroe

1983 - P. Fleming and J. P McEnroe
T. E. Gullikson and T. R. Gullikson

1984 - P. Fleming and J. P. McEnroe
P. Cash and P. McNamee

1985 - H. P. Guenthardt and B. Taroczy
P. Cash and J. B. Fitzgerald

1986 - J. Nystrom and M. Wilander
G. Donnelly and P. Fleming

1987 - K. Flach and R. Seguso
S. Casal and E. Sanchez

1988 - K. Flach and R. Seguso
J. B. Fitzgerald and A. Jarryd

1989 - J. B. Fitzgerald and A. Jarryd
R. Leach and J. Pugh

1990 - R. Leach and J. Pugh
P. Aldrich and D. T. Visser

1991 - J. B. Fitzgerald and A. Jarryd
J. Frana and L. Lavalle

1992 - J. P. McEnroe and M. Stich
J. Grabb and R. A. Reneberg

1993 - T. A. Woodbridge and M. Woodforde
G. Connell and P. Galbraith

1994 - T. A. Woodbridge and M. Woodforde
G. Connell and P. Galbraith

1995 - T. A. Woodbridge and M. Woodforde
R. Leach and S. Melville

1996 - T. A. Woodbridge and M. Woodforde
B. Black and G. Connell

LADIES' DOUBLES

1913 - Mrs. R. J. McNair and Miss D. P. Boothby
Mrs. A, Sterry and Mrs. Lambert Chambers

1914 - Miss E. Ryan and Miss A. M. Morton
Mrs. D. R. Larcombe and Mrs. F. J. Hannam

1919 - Mlle. S. Lenglen and Miss E. Ryan
Mrs. Lambert Chambers and Mrs. D. R. Larcombe

1920 - Mlle. S. Lenglen and Miss E. Ryan
Mrs. Lambert Chambers and Mrs. D. R. Larcombe

1921 - Mlle. S. Lenglen and Miss E. Ryan
Mrs. A. E. Beamish and Mrs. G. E. Peacock

1922 - Mlle. S. Lenglen and Miss E. Ryan
Mrs. A. D. Stocks and Miss K. McKane

1923 - Mlle. S. Lenglen and Miss E. Ryan
Miss J. Austin and Miss E. L. Colyer

1924 - Mrs. H. Wightman and Miss H. Wills
Mrs. B. C. Covell and Miss K. McKane

1925 - Mlle. S. Lenglen and Miss E. Ryan
Mrs. A. V. Bridge and Mrs. C. G. McIlquham

1926 - Miss E. Ryan and Miss M. K. Browne
Mrs. L. A. Godfree and Miss E. L. Colyer

1927 - Miss H. Wills and Miss E. Ryan
Miss E. L. Heine and Mrs. G. E. Peacock

1928 - Mrs. Holcroft-Watson and Miss P. Saunders
Miss E. H. Harvey and Miss E. Bennett

1929 - Mrs. Holcroft-Watson and Mrs. L. R. C. Michell
Mrs. B. C. Covell and Mrs. D. C. Shepherd-Barron

1930 - Mrs. F. S. Moody and Miss E. Ryan
Miss E. Cross and Miss S. Palfrey

1931 - Mrs. D. C. Shepherd-Barron and Miss P. E. Mudford
Mlle. D. Metaxa and Mlle. J. Sigart

1932 - Mlle. D. Metaxa and Mlle. J. Sigart
Miss E. Ryan and Miss H. H. Jacobs

1933 - Mme. R. Mathieu and Miss E. Ryan
Miss F. James and Miss A. M. Yorke

1934 - Mme. R. Mathieu and Miss E. Ryan
Mrs. D. Andrus and Mme. S. Henrotin

1935 - Miss F. James and Miss K. E. Stammers
Mme. R. Mathieu and Frau. S. Sperling

1936 - Miss F. James and Miss K. E. Stammers
Mrs. S. P. Fabyan and Miss H. H. Jacobs

1937 - Mme. R. Mathieu and Miss A. M. Yorke
Mrs. M. R. King and Mrs. J. B. Pittman

1938 - Mrs. S. P. Fabyan and Miss A. Marble
Mme. R. Mathieu and Miss A. M. Yorke

1939 - Mrs. S. P. Fabyan and Miss A. Marble
Miss H. H. Jacobs and Miss A. M. Yorke

1946 - Miss L. Brough and Miss M. Osborne
Miss P. Betz and Miss D. Hart

1947 - Miss D. Hart and Mrs. P. C. Todd
Miss L. Brough and Miss M. Osborne

1948 - Miss L. Brough and Mrs. W. du Pont
Miss D. Hart and Mrs. P. C. Todd

1949 - Miss L. Brough and Mrs. W. du Pont
Miss G. Moran and Mrs. P. C. Todd

1950 - Miss L. Brough and Mrs. W. du Pont
Miss S. Fry and Miss D. Hart

1951 - Miss S. Fry and Miss D. Hart
Miss L. Brough and Mrs. W. du Pont

1952 - Miss S. Fry and Miss D. Hart
Miss L. Brough and Miss M. Connolly

1953 - Miss S. Fry and Miss D. Hart
Miss M. Connolly and Miss J. Sampson

1954 - Miss L. Brough and Mrs. W. du Pont
Miss S. Fry and Miss D. Hart

1955 - Miss A. Mortimer and Miss J. A. Shilcock
Miss S. J. Bloomer and Miss P. E. Ward

1956 - Miss A. Buxton and Miss A. Gibson
Miss F. Muller and Miss D. G. Seeney

1957 - Miss A. Gibson and Miss D. R. Hard
Mrs. K. Hawton and Mrs. T. D. Long

1958 - Miss M. E. Bueno and Miss A. Gibson
Mrs. W. du Pont and Miss M. Varner

1959 - Miss J. Arth and Miss D. R. Hard
Mrs. J. G. Fleitz and Miss C. C. Truman

1960 - Miss M. E. Bueno and Miss D. R. Hard
Miss S. Reynolds and Miss R. Schuurman

1961 - Miss K. Hantze and Miss B. J. Moffitt
Miss J. Lehane and Miss M. Smith

1962 - Miss B. J. Moffitt and Mrs. J. R. Susman
Mrs. L. E. G. Price and Miss R. Schuurman

1963 - Miss M. E. Bueno and Miss D. R. Hard
Miss R. A. Ebbern and Miss M. Smith

1964 - Miss M. Smith and Miss L. R. Turner
Miss B. J. Moffitt and Mrs. J. R. Susman

1965 - Miss M. E. Bueno and Miss B. J. Moffitt
Miss F. Durr and Miss J. Lieffrig

1966 - Miss M. E. Bueno and Miss N. Richey
Miss M. Smith and Miss J. A. M. Tegart

1967 - Miss R. Casals and Mrs. L. W. King
Miss M. E. Bueno and Miss N. Richey

1968 - Miss R. Casals and Mrs. L. W. King
Miss F. Durr and Mrs. P. F. Jones

1969 - Mrs. B. M. Court and Miss J. A. M. Tegart
Miss P. S. A. Hogan and Miss M. Michel

1970 - Miss R. Casals and Mrs. L. W. King
Miss F. Durr and Miss S. V. Wade

1971 - Miss R. Casals and Mrs. L. W. King
Mrs. B. M. Court and Miss E. F. Goolagong

1972 - Mrs. L. W. King and Miss B. F. Stove
Mrs. D. E. Dalton and Miss F. Durr

1973 - Miss R. Casals and Mrs. L. W. King
Miss F. Durr and Miss B. F. Stove

1974 - Miss E. F. Goolagong and Miss M. Michel
Miss H. F. Gourlay and Miss K. M. Krantzcke

1975 - Miss A. Kiyomura and Miss K. Sawamatsu
Miss F. Durr and Miss B. F. Stove

1976 - Miss C. M. Evert and Miss M. Navratilova
Mrs. L. W. King and Miss B. F. Stove

1977 - Mrs. H. F. Gourlay Cawley and Miss J. C. Russell
Miss M. Navratilova and Miss B. F . Stove

1978 - Mrs. G. E. Reid and Miss. W. M. Turnbull
Miss M. Jausovec and Miss V. Ruzici

1979 - Mrs. L. W. King and Miss M. Navratilova
Miss B. F. Stove and Miss W. M. Turnbull

1980 - Miss K. Jordan and Miss A. E. Smith
Miss R. Casals and Miss W. M. Turnbull

1981 - Miss M. Navratilova and Miss P. H. Shriver
Miss K. Jordan and Miss A. E. Smith

1982 - Miss M. Navratilova and Miss P. H. Shriver
Miss K. Jordan and Miss A. E. Smith

1983 - Miss M. Navratilova and Miss P. H. Shriver
Miss R. Casals and Miss W. M. Turnbull

1984 - Miss M. Navratilova and Miss P. H. Shriver
Miss K. Jordan and Miss A. E. Smith

1985 - Miss K. Jordan and Mrs. P. D. Smylie
Miss M. Navratilova and Miss P. H. Shriver

1986 - Miss M. Navratilova and Miss P. H. Shriver
Miss H. Mandlikova and Miss W. M. Turnbull

1987 - Miss C. Kohde-Kilsch and Miss H. Sukova
Miss B. Nagelsen and Mrs. P. D. Smylie

1988 - Miss S. Graf and Miss G. Sabatini
Miss L. Savchenko and Miss N. Zvereva

1989 - Miss J. Novotna and Miss H. Sukova
Miss L. Savchenko and Miss N. Zvereva

1990 - Miss J. Novotna and Miss H. Sukova
Miss K. Jordan and Mrs. P. D. Smylie

1991 - Miss L. Savchenko and Miss N. Zvereva
Miss G. Fernandez and Miss J. Novotna

1992 - Miss G. Fernandez and Miss N. Zvereva
Miss J. Novotna and Mrs. L. Savchenko-Neiland

1993 - Miss G. Fernandez and Miss N. Zvereva
Mrs. L. Neiland and Miss J. Novotna

1994 - Miss G. Fernandez and Miss N. Zvereva
Miss J. Novotna and Miss A. Sanchez Vicario

1995 - Miss J. Novotna and Miss A. Sanchez Vicario
Miss G. Fernandez and Miss N. Zvereva

1996 - Miss M. Hingis and Miss H. Sukova
Miss M.J. McGrath and Mrs. L. Neiland

MIXED DOUBLES

1913 – Hope Crisp and Mrs. C. O. Tuckey *J. C. Parke and Mrs. D. R. Larcombe*	1948 – J. E. Bromwich and Miss L. Brough *F. A. Sedgman and Miss D. Hart*	1973 – O. K. Davidson and Mrs. L. W. King *R. Ramirez and Miss J. S. Newberry*
1914 – J. C. Parke and Mrs. D.R. Larcombe *A. F. Wilding and Mlle. M. Broquedis*	1949 – E. W. Sturgess and Mrs. S. P. Summers *J. E. Bromwich and Miss L. Brough*	1974 – O. K. Davidson and Mrs. L. W. King *M. J. Farrell and Miss L. J. Charles*
1919 – R. Lycett and Miss E. Ryan *A. D. Prebble and Mrs. Lambert Chambers*	1950 – E. W. Sturgess and Miss L. Brough *G. E. Brown and Mrs. P. C. Todd*	1975 – M. C. Riessen and Mrs. B. M. Court *A. J. Stone and Miss B. F. Stove*
1920 – G. L. Patterson and Mlle. S. Lenglen *R. Lycett and Miss E. Ryan*	1951 – F. A. Sedgman and Miss D. Hart *M. G. Rose and Mrs. N. M. Bolton*	1976 – A. D. Roche and Miss F. Durr *R. L. Stockton and Miss R. Casals*
1921 – R. Lycett and Miss E. Ryan *M. Woosnam and Miss P. L. Howkins*	1952 – F. A. Sedgman and Miss D. Hart *E. Morea and Mrs. T. D. Long*	1977 – R. A. J. Hewitt and Miss G. R. Stevens *F. D. McMillan and Miss B. F. Stove*
1922 – P. O'Hara–Wood and Mlle. S. Lenglen *R. Lycett and Miss E. Ryan*	1953 – V. Seixas and Miss D. Hart *E. Morea and Miss S. Fry*	1978 – F. D. McMillan and Miss B. F. Stove *R. O. Ruffels and Mrs. L. W. King*
1923 – R. Lycett and Miss E. Ryan *L. S. Deane and Mrs. D. C. Shepherd-Barron*	1954 – V. Seixas and Miss D. Hart *K. R. Rosewall and Mrs. W. du Pont*	1979 – R. A. J. Hewitt and Miss G. R. Stevens *F. D. McMillan and Miss B. F. Stove*
1924 – J. B. Gilbert and Miss K. McKane *L. A. Godfree and Mrs. D. C. Shepherd-Barron*	1955 – V. Seixas and Miss D. Hart *E. Morea and Miss A. Gibson*	1980 – J. R. Austin and Miss T. Austin *M. R. Edmondson and Miss D. L. Fromholtz*
1925 – J. Borotra and Mlle. S. Lenglen *H. L. de Morpurgo and Miss E. Ryan*	1956 – V. Seixas and Miss S. Fry *G. Mulloy and Miss A. Gibson*	1981 – F. D. McMillan and Miss B. F. Stove *J. R. Austin and Miss T. Austin*
1926 – L. A. Godfree and Mrs. L. A. Godfree *H. Kinsey and Miss M. K. Browne*	1957 – M. G. Rose and Miss D. R. Hard *N. A. Fraser and Miss A. Gibson*	1982 – K. Curren and Miss A. E. Smith *J. M. Lloyd and Miss W. M. Turnbull*
1927 – F. T. Hunter and Miss E. Ryan *L. A. Godfree and Mrs. L. A. Godfree*	1958 – R. N. Howe and Miss L. Coghlan *K. Nielsen and Miss A. Gibson*	1983 – J. M. Lloyd and Miss W. M. Turnbull *S. Denton and Mrs. L. W. King*
1928 – P. D. B. Spence and Miss E. Ryan *J. Crawford and Miss D. Akhurst*	1959 – R. Laver and Miss D. R. Hard *N. A. Fraser and Miss M. E. Bueno*	1984 – J. M. Lloyd and Miss W. M. Turnbull *S. Denton and Miss K. Jordan*
1929 – F. T. Hunter and Miss H. Wills *I. G. Collins and Miss J. Fry*	1960 – R. Laver and Miss D. R. Hard *R. N. Howe and Miss M. E. Bueno*	1985 – P. McNamee and Miss M. Navratilova *J. B. Fitzgerald and Mrs. P. D. Smylie*
1930 – J. H. Crawford and Miss E. Ryan *D. Prenn and Fraulein H. Krahwinkel*	1961 – F. S. Stolle and Miss L. R. Turner *R. N. Howe and Miss E. Buding*	1986 – K. Flach and Miss K. Jordan *H. P. Guenthardt and Miss M. Navratilova*
1931 – G. M. Lott and Mrs L. A. Harper *I. G. Collins and Miss J. C. Ridley*	1962 – N. A. Fraser and Mrs. W. du Pont *R. D. Ralston and Miss A. S. Haydon*	1987 – M. J. Bates and Miss J. M. Durie *D. Cahill and Miss N. Provis*
1932 – E. Maier and Miss E. Ryan *H. C. Hopman and Mlle. J. Sigart*	1963 – K. N. Fletcher and Miss M. Smith *R. A. J. Hewitt and Miss D. R. Hard*	1988 – S. E. Stewart and Miss Z. L. Garrison *K. Jones and Mrs. S. W. Magers*
1933 – G. von Cramm and Fraulein H. Krahwinkel *N. G. Farquharson and Miss M. Heeley*	1964 – F. S. Stolle and Miss L. R. Turner *K. N. Fletcher and Miss M. Smith*	1989 – J. Pugh and Miss J. Novotna *M. Kratzmann and Miss J. M. Byrne*
1934 – R. Miki and Miss D. E. Round *H. W. Austin and Mrs D. C. Shepherd-Barron*	1965 – K. N. Fletcher and Miss M. Smith *A. D. Roche and Miss J. A. M. Tegart*	1990 – R. Leach and Miss Z. L. Garrison *J. B. Fitzgerald and Mrs P. D. Smylie*
1935 – F. J. Perry and Miss D. E. Round *H. C. Hopman and Mrs. H. C. Hopman*	1966 – K. N. Fletcher and Miss M. Smith *R. D. Ralston and Mrs. L. W. King*	1991 – J. B. Fitzgerald and Mrs. P. D. Smylie *J. Pugh and Miss N. Zvereva*
1936 – F. J. Perry and Miss D. E. Round *J. D. Budge and Miss S. P. Fabyan*	1967 – O. K. Davidson and Mrs. L. W. King *K. N. Fletcher and Miss M. E. Bueno*	1992 – C. Suk and Mrs L. Savchenko–Neiland *J. Eltingh and Miss M. Oremans*
1937 – J. D. Budge and Miss A. Marble *Y. Petra and Mme. R. Mathieu*	1968 – K. N. Fletcher and Mrs. B. M. Court *A. Metreveli and Miss O. Morozova*	1993 – M. Woodforde and Miss M. Navratilova *T. Nijssen and Miss M. M. Bollegraf*
1938 – J. D. Budge and Miss A. Marble *H. Henkel and Mrs. S. P. Fabyan*	1969 – F. S. Stolle and Mrs. P. F. Jones *A. D. Roche and Miss J. A. M. Tegart*	1994 – T. A. Woodbridge and Miss H. Sukova *T. J. Middleton and Miss L. M. McNeil*
1939 – R. L. Riggs and Miss A. Marble *F. H. D. Wilde and Miss N. B. Brown*	1970 – I. Nastase and Miss R. Casals *A. Metreveli and Miss O. Morozova*	1995 – J. Stark and Miss M. Navratilova *C. Suk and Miss G. Fernandez*
1946 – T. Brown and Miss L. Brough *G. E. Brown and Miss D. Bundy*	1971 – O. K. Davidson and Mrs. L. W. King *M. C. Riessen and Mrs. B. M. Court*	1996 – C. Suk and Miss H. Sukova *M. Woodforde and Mrs. L. Neiland*
1947 – J. E. Bromwich and Miss L. Brough *C. F. Long and Mrs. N. M. Bolton*	1972 – I. Nastase and Miss R. Casals *K.G. Warwick and Miss E. F. Goolagong*	

THE JUNIOR CHAMPIONSHIP ROLL

BOYS' SINGLES

1947 – K. Nielsen (Denmark)	1959 – T. Lejus (U.S.S.R.)	1972 – B. Borg (Sweden)	1985 – L. Lavalle (Mexico)
1948 – S. Stockenberg (Sweden)	1960 – A. R. Mandelstam (S.A.)	1973 – W. Martin (U.S.A.)	1986 – E. Velez (Mexico)
1949 – S. Stockenberg (Sweden)	1961 – C. E. Graebner (U.S.A.)	1974 – W. Martin (U.S.A.)	1987 – D. Nargiso (Italy)
1950 – J. A. T. Horn (G.B.)	1962 – S. Matthews (G.B.)	1975 – C. J. Lewis (N.Z.)	1988 – N. Pereira (Venezuela)
1951 – J. Kupferburger (S.A.)	1963 – N. Kalogeropoulos (Greece)	1976 – H. Guenthardt (Switzerland)	1989 – N. Kulti (Sweden)
1952 – R. K. Wilson (G.B.)	1964 – I. El Shafei (U.A.R.)	1977 – V. A. Winitsky (U.S.A.)	1990 – L. Paes (India)
1953 – W. A. Knight (G.B.)	1965 – V. Korotkov (U.S.S.R.)	1978 – I. Lendl (Czechoslovakia)	1991 – T. Enquist (Sweden)
1954 – R. Krishnan (India)	1966 – V. Korotkov (U.S.S.R.)	1979 – R. Krishnan (India)	1992 – D. Skoch (Czechoslovakia)
1955 – M. P. Hann (G.B.)	1967 – M. Orantes (Spain)	1980 – T. Tulasne (France)	1993 – R. Sabau (Romania)
1956 – R. Holmberg (U.S.A.)	1968 – J. G. Alexander (Australia)	1981 – M. W. Anger (U.S.A.)	1994 – S. Humphries (U.S.A.)
1957 – J. I. Tattersall (G.B.)	1969 – B. Bertram (S.A.)	1982 – P. Cash (Australia)	1995 – O. Mutis (France)
1958 – E. Buchholz (U.S.A.)	1970 – B. Bertram (S.A.)	1983 – S. Edberg (Sweden)	1996 – V. Voltchkov (Belarus)
	1971 – R. Kreiss (U.S.A.)	1984 – M.Kratzmann (Australia)	

BOYS' DOUBLES

1982 – P. Cash and J. Frawley	1987 – J. Stoltenberg and T. Woodbridge	1992 – S. Baldas and S. Draper
1983 – M. Kratzmann and S. Youl	1988 – J. Stoltenberg and T. Woodbridge	1993 – S. Downs and J. Greenhalgh
1984 – R. Brown and R. Weiss	1989 – J. Palmer and J. Stark	1994 – B. Ellwood and M. Philippoussis
1985 – A. Moreno and J. Yzaga	1990 – S. Lareau and S. Leblanc	1995 – M. Lee and J.M. Trotman
1986 – T. Carbonell and P. Korda	1991 – K. Alami and G. Rusedski	1996 – D. Bracciali and J. Robichaud

GIRLS' SINGLES

1948 – Miss O. Miskova (Czechoslovakia)	1960 – Miss K. Hantze (U.S.A.)	1973 – Miss A. Kiyomura (U.S.A.)	1986 – Miss N. Zvereva (U.S.S.R.)
1949 – Miss C. Mercelis (Belgium)	1961 – Miss G. Baksheeva (U.S.S.R.)	1974 – Miss M. Jausovec (Yugoslavia)	1987 – Miss N. Zvereva (U.S.S.R.)
1950 – Miss L. Cornell (G.B.)	1962 – Miss G. Baksheeva (U.S.S.R.)	1975 – Miss N. Y. Chmyreva (U.S.S.R.)	1988 – Miss B. Schultz (Netherlands)
1951 – Miss L. Cornell (G.B.)	1963 – Miss D. M. Salfati (France)	1976 – Miss N. Y. Chmyreva (U.S.S.R.)	1989 – Miss A. Strnadova (Czechoslavakia)
1952 – Miss ten Bosch (Netherlands)	1964 – Miss P. Bartkowicz (U.S.A.)	1977 – Miss L. Antonoplis (U.S.A.)	1990 – Miss A. Strnadova (Czechoslavakia)
1953 – Miss D. Kilian (S.A.)	1965 – Miss O. Morozova (U.S.S.R.)	1978 – Miss T. Austin (U.S.A.)	1991 – Miss B. Rittner (Germany)
1954 – Miss V. A. Pitt (G.B.)	1966 – Miss B. Lindstrom (Finland)	1979 – Miss M. L. Piatek (U.S.A.)	1992 – Miss C. Rubin (U.S.A.)
1955 – Miss S. M. Armstrong (G.B.)	1967 – Miss J. Salome (Netherlands)	1980 – Miss D. Freeman (Australia)	1993 – Miss N. Feber (Belgium)
1956 – Miss A. S. Haydon (G.B.)	1968 – Miss K. Pigeon (U.S.A.)	1981 – Miss Z. Garrison (U.S.A.)	1994 – Miss M. Hingis (Switzerland)
1957 – Miss M. Arnold (U.S.A.)	1969 – Miss K. Sawamatsu (Japan)	1982 – Miss C. Tanvier (France)	1995 – Miss A. Olsza (Poland)
1958 – Miss S. M. Moore (U.S.A.)	1970 – Miss S. Walsh (U.S.A.)	1983 – Miss P. Paradis (France)	1996 – Miss A. Mauresmo (France)
1959 – Miss J. Cross (S.A.)	1971 – Miss M. Kroschina (U.S.S.R.)	1984 – Miss A. N. Croft (G.B.)	
	1972 – Miss I. Kloss (S.A.)	1985 – Miss A. Holikova (Czechoslovakia)	

GIRLS' DOUBLES

1982 – Miss B. Herr and Miss P. Barg	1987 – Miss N. Medvedeva and Miss N. Zvereva	1992 – Miss M. Avotins and Miss L. McShea
1983 – Miss P. Fendick and Miss P. Hy	1988 – Miss J. A. Faull and Miss R. McQuillan	1993 – Miss L. Courtois and Miss N. Feber
1984 – Miss C. Kuhlman and Miss S. Rehe	1989 – Miss J. Capriati and Miss M. McGrath	1994 – Miss E. De Villiers and Miss E. E. Jelfs
1985 – Miss L. Field and Miss J. Thompson	1990 – Miss K. Habsudova and Miss A. Strnadova	1995 – Miss C. Black and Miss A. Olsza
1986 – Miss M. Jaggard and Miss L. O'Neill	1991 – Miss C. Barclay and Miss L. Zaltz	1996 – Miss O. Barabanschikova and Miss A. Mauresmo